Dr. Norman Cawfield

Reconstructing
YOUR
PERSONALITY

RECONSTRUCTING YOUR PERSONALITY
God's Plan For Happiness And Success

Dr. Norman C. Cawfield
104 Queen Street West
Brampton, Ontario L6X 1A4

Copyright © 1985 by Dr. Norman C. Cawfield
Printed in the United States of America

Editorial assistance by Stephen R. Clark
Writing & Creative Services
P.O. Box 1443
Findlay, Ohio 45839-1443

Prepared for Whitaker House by Valeria Cindric

CONTENTS

DEDICATION

This book is dedicated to my wife Holly for demonstrating to me consistent love and approval; to my daughter, Katie, who is a lovely reflection of her mother; to my parents for their godliness and faithfulness; and to all those friends, colleagues, and patients who have helped mold these principles into reality and have loved me in return.

These are my greatest assets.

FOREWORD

Strength, compassion, dedication, wisdom, integrity—these are qualities that come to mind when I consider Dr. Norman Cawfield. But most of all, he is a man of God.

In his profession he has treated my sons, Reynold and Ron, most skillfully. Throughout their high school and college football careers, Dr. Cawfield's hands helped minister physical wholeness.

But this doctor has wide-ranging concerns that reach far beyond his chiropractic practice. This book is the result. Here is a ministry to spirit, soul, mind, and body—as well as to the whole spectrum of human relations.

Reconstructing Your Personality will minister truth by the power of the Holy Spirit to enable you to truly keep what Jesus declared to be the first and second great commandments of God: *"Thou shalt have no other gods before me"* (Exodus 20:3) and *"Thou shalt love thy neighbour as thyself"* (Mark 12:31).

David Mainse
President, *100 Huntley Street*

INTRODUCTION

In any discussion related to the complexities of the human personality, we must first make some very basic assumptions.

To understand man from a Christian perspective, we must agree:

1. That a Supreme Designer exists.

2. That this Designer's plan for man was interrupted by man's free-will rebellion against His purposes.

3. That the Designer wished to reestablish a relationship with man, but His character demanded that someone bear the penalty for man's rebellion.

4. In Jesus Christ, God found One who possessed no rebellion and was willing, through love, to submit to the penalty for man's actions by surrendering His life for man.

5. Through Jesus Christ, man was ushered once again into right relationship with God.

6. Through the death and resurrection of Jesus Christ, healing, wholeness, peace, blessing, and the

promise of abundant life were made available to mankind.

My intention is to help wholeness and healing enter the lives of all who read this book. I pray that God, by His Holy Spirit, will touch you and heal those areas of your life that need changing.

It takes courage to have your life challenged by God's Word. But in the light of God's revelation, you can interpret your actions and identify negative emotions. Then, by God's grace and the power of the Holy Spirit, you can be changed to live an abundant, joy-filled life.

Choose today to tap God's potential! He can reconstruct your life and your personality if you will let Him.

Self-Analysis Questionnaire

Throughout this book there are questions and exercises that require your participation. You may want to use a notebook to record your answers and keep as an indication of your progress.

This first list of questions is very important because they will help you evaluate yourself in relation to your present attitudes. Be as honest and candid as possible. Take your time and answer each question thoroughly.

1. What do you believe is your most powerful asset?

2. What, in your mind, short circuits your power with God?

3. What personality weaknesses or complexes are you dealing with?

4. What is your life's dream or your greatest prayer?

5. What frightens you the most about life?

6. Did you ever fail? Have you forgiven yourself? Have you learned from your mistake?

7. What was your most selfless act? Did others appreciate it? Why?

8. Do you hold hatred for anyone? Why?

9. Are you afraid of a particular person? Why?

10. Are you a kind and thoughtful servant to others?

11. Are you perhaps too demanding of everyone else? Why?

12. Have you learned to forgive and bless others instead?

13. Who has been the most influential person in your life?

14. Are you realistic about life or are you a daydreamer?

15. Are you totally honest with others as well as yourself?

16. Do you put on a facade most of the time, or can you relax and "be yourself"?

17. Do you learn through failure or become discouraged after defeat?

18. What do you hope to achieve in life?

19. How are you going to reach your final destination?

20. Have you fully taken stock of and utilized all your abilities, or are you wasting your time and talents?
21. Do you desire to live an abundant life—one that will please God through obedience and discipline?
22. Do you like yourself? Do you have a desire to change and grow as a person?
23. Could you leave this world today and enter eternity in peace?

Chapter 1

HOW YOUR PERSONALITY DEVELOPS

Have you ever heard someone say, "She may not be much to look at, but she has a great personality"? Do some people have more personality than others?

Everyone has a unique, God-given personality, endowed with special talents, gifts, and abilities. In addition, the characteristics of God's own personality are instilled within each one of us because we are created in His image.

Although you were created in the image of God, that image has been damaged and broken over the years. From the day you were born into this sinful world, your personality has been bombarded by positive and negative influences. The positive influences—loving parents, stimulating environment, adequate nourishment—have attributed to the formation of the positive aspects of your personality.

On the other hand, the negative influences—verbal or physical abuse, failure, sickness—have created gapping holes in the wall of your personality. Certain foundational blocks may have been damaged, throwing the entire structure of your character off balance.

No one gets through life without some harm being done to his personality. God wants to restore your broken personality and rebuild your character in His image and with His nature.

The character of God is displayed for us in the person of Jesus Christ. He is the reflection of God's personality. The wonderful message of the gospel is that you have the potential to take on the personality of Jesus Christ and become Christlike in your attitudes and behavior.

Many people go through life never realizing the tremendous potential available to them through God's Spirit. Jesus gave His Holy Spirit to help us become all that God created us to be—like Jesus.

"How can I become like Jesus?" you may be asking. That's where reconstruction of your personality comes in.

Self-Image Makers

When searching for a way to bring about permanent change, some people are fooled into thinking that the answer lies somewhere outside themselves. They keep searching for pills, potions, prescriptions, and easy "fixes." As a result they never find complete, permanent healing—only the illusion of healing.

God's psychiatry, however, has the answer that will make you completely whole. His divine principles can heal the innermost part of your personality. What part of your inner life needs to be reconstructed?

Sometimes the most difficult aspect of personality reconstruction is not the healing but the identification of the areas of our lives that need to be healed.

The innermost part of your personality is made up of your most secret and personal thoughts, impressions, and interpretations of the world around you. This unseen part of you is different from the outer personality viewed by other people.

The hidden attitudes of your heart form the innermost part of your personality. These attitudes are a by-product of all the events, tragedies, successes, etc. that program your future interpretation of life occurances. They filter and explain reality in terms of learned, programmed impulses, giving you either a proper perspective or a distorted view of life. Most people need to have the dominant, binding attitudes of their innermost personality changed by the power of God.

Traumatic or unpleasant experiences can produce fear, anxiety, and confusion. You may have experienced some trauma while still in your mother's womb. A pre-born infant senses sadness, rejection, pain, and loneliness that can result in pre-conscious fears and hurts. These negative influences damage a child's personality and can affect how he reacts to certain situations throughout his lifetime.

In the maturing process from infancy through

childhood, many factors wear and tear on our personalities. In the family situation, our siblings can be the most sarcastic and critical people we encounter. Many adults are afraid to talk to strangers or afraid to speak in public because of criticism and fear planted in them by sibling rivalry long ago. It isn't their fault, yet the fear they are carrying is keeping them from fulfilling God's purpose for their lives. They've put up walls and barriers that God needs to pull down.

Peer Pressure

Peer pressure is another powerful, molding force—especially during the developing stages of our lives. Embarrassing or degrading experiences during our school years can affect our performance and self-image as adults.

As long as I can remember, I have always loved music. When I was in second grade, I joined Miss Jelly's choir and was chosen to sing a solo part at a special assembly. A little first-grade girl and I were to alternately sing the verses of the *Twenty-Third Psalm*. It was a great honor to be selected to perform before the entire school body.

The day came, and I nervously watched the classes file into the auditorium. When I saw my tough, second-grade buddies staring up at me from their seats on the back row, I suddenly became extremely embarrassed.

Having a high soprano voice in my large frame

was humiliating enough, but then something happened to make matters even worse. After the little girl sang, I opened my mouth and realized my voice was even higher than hers!

Fortunately, my buddies were merciful and did not tease me badly about my performance. If they had seen the opportunity to attack my vulnerability, I would probably have collapsed into a pile of ashes. After this experience, I made an inner vow never to put myself in a situation like that again. It has taken years for me to be healed of the impact of that traumatic event.

Are there embarrassing incidents in your past that are keeping you from performing up to your potential in the present?

When Chuck was a child, his grade school class presented the play *Robin Hood*. He had long been fascinated with this romantic character and began to imagine himself playing the lead role as the dashing and daring hero. Chuck could see himself as the champion, living in the forest, hunting wild game for food, and helping poor people.

As the teacher began choosing children for the various roles, she came to the character of Friar Tuck—the fat, clumsy clergyman who bumbles his way through the entire story. To this day Chuck can remember her pausing as she asked, "And who can we get to play Friar Tuck?"

Everyone in the class immediately turned and looked at him. "Chuck!" they shouted in unison. It was unanimous. They considered him perfect for what he thought was the most repugnant part in the production. From that time on, Chuck was marked and teased. For years he saw himself as a "Friar Tuck" kind of person—fat, somewhat dull, thick-headed, and clumsy.

That little incident could have molded a wrong but lasting self-image in Chuck. It could have falsely impressed certain limitations upon him.

You can probably recall similar incidents in your own life. Have you ever felt that you were unanimously chosen for a repugnant role in life?

A teasing remark or a misunderstanding that is truly believed may later become reality in a person's life. Psychologists claim that about half of our mental and emotional energy each day is spent repressing painful memories.

God wants to break through these misconceptions and hurts. He wants to heal those painful parts of your personality.

Some little hurts remain little, yet many little hurts can accumulate into big problems. Other hurts start small and grow large, sometimes becoming more and more menacing. Your imagination, if allowed to dwell on the past, can be your worst enemy.

The Power Of The Past

Most of us fail to realize how our pasts influence our present problems because we are wrapped up in the concerns of the moment. We drag around the weight of bad memories and unpleasant experiences, crippling ourselves without being aware of it.

Rick was a young man who attended my seminars on "Healing for the Personality." Having lived for years with an alcoholic mother who beat him constantly, Rick was driven to an overwhelming state of insecurity. He was literally obsessed with certain beliefs that manipulated his actions. He believed that by repeating certain behavior he could control the circumstances in his life. These actions eventually developed into complex rituals which he felt bound to perform perfectly.

If one day, for example, Rick drew a correlation between tying his shoes in a certain fashion and success for that day, he would adopt that pattern routinely. This practice would relieve the deep-seated need for security within him. In counseling, I discovered that Rick had a habit of having to touch every telephone pole or every crack in the pavement when he went for a walk, otherwise he would be overcome by anxiety. These compulsive acts represented a deep need for reconstruction of the innermost part of his personality.

Christ is Lord of the past, the present, and the future. He is Lord over every season of our lives, not just Lord of this or that fragment of time.

Modern psychologists, however, emphasize only the past, without equipping a person with insight to deal with the present. Or, they place all the emphasis on the present and living for the moment, while disregarding the powerful influence of the past. In both cases, a person's spiritual self, which is eternal, is ignored.

Healing For The Past

One popular psychological trend used in counseling people with phobias or uncontrolled behavior is *behavior modification.* This method, however, deals solely with the external manifestations of the personality. The present crisis is averted without realizing its potential ramifications on the innermost personality.

God can heal the past scars in your innermost personality. He will empower you to deal with your present circumstances, enabling you to look with confidence and courage toward the future. God can remove the sting of the past and turn the dread of tomorrow into joyful anticipation. An attitude of praise replaces the spirit of heaviness.

Why does the innermost personality need to be healed?

You have been programmed to respond to the present by sensitivities, complexes, inferiorities, and so on, generated from events in your past. At some time in your life you were cut emotionally, and you allowed the wound to go untreated and to fester. Now you are infected with bitterness and hostility.

You may have been born again at an early age, but memories from previous experiences could be lurking in the shadows of your mind. When you accept Jesus Christ as your Savior, your spirit is immediately made new. But it takes time for your mind and emotions to be completely healed. An illness cannot be cured after only one treatment, and your personality cannot be reconstructed at the moment of salvation. The process of sanctification, spiritual maturity, and reconstruction of the personality is an ongoing, lifetime process.

Any healing requires time plus care and discipline. Your present behavior, whether you are aware of it or not, is conditioned by memories buried in your innermost personality. The way you think about yourself, the way you act toward others, and the way you feel in various situations is influenced by your memory. In fact, your memory determines how you perceive yourself in relation to your environment.

Your Mental Recorder

Where do memories come from? Your memory can be thought of as a "mental tape recorder." In a sense, the mind has two of these mental recorders. One represents the conscious level—the realm of awareness. The second represents the innermost part of your personality—the hidden realm where many unpleasant experiences have been repressed.

Your immediate thoughts are stored on the first recorder, your *conscious* mind. Most of your pleasant memories are also stored here. All of your experiences are first recorded in the conscious—this is where the live action takes place. When something unpleasant happens, you "erase" it from your conscious and "transfer" it to the *subconscious* part of your mind. Nothing is ever lost; it is only moved from one "recorder" to the other.

Think of your *consciousness* as the living room of your mind. Here is where daily events take place. The *subconsciousness*, however, is like the attic. Older memories are stored there, where they gather dust and remain neglected. When something you don't like occurs in the living room, it gets shoved into your attic memory.

The old adage, "out of sight, out of mind," however, does not apply to our memories. Unpleasant experiences can be suppressed from immediate consciousness, but they are still in your memory. They affect your life whether you are aware of their presence or not. All of your past—good and bad, pleasant and unpleasant—influences how you behave today. Your past always impacts on your present.

I counseled with a teenager whose father had always told him how worthless he was. This father had harassed the child, constantly complaining that he could never do anything right. When the boy was still very young, his father died. The boy's mother, a very patient and understanding woman, raised her son in an atmosphere of love and concern. Yet, as the boy grew older, he continually had problems in school. Although he seemed bright and alert, his grades were low. Neither his mother nor his counselors and teachers at school could figure out why he consistently failed in spite of his obvious ability.

What was wrong with the boy? Although the son could not recall clearly what life had been like when his father was alive, this teenager's memories were full of his father's put-downs. When faced with academic challenges, the boy felt inadequate and worthless. His subconscious was "playing back" the poor self-image instilled in him by his father. It affected the boy's performance in the present.

Even a person who has led a successful life for many years and has established a good career can suddenly be faced with a perplexing dilemma. A new situation, similar to a past experience that is submerged in the inner personality, can crop up and cause failure in the present.

While you have forgotten the details stored in your innermost personality, the devil hasn't. He will work to keep those subconscious "tapes" repressed, while at the same time using the negative feelings of those situations to create problems for you now.

The old subconscious tapes are still dictating failure, disease, grief, self-pity, and condemnation. They have done this for so long that they have become deeply ingrained within your personality. Jesus wants to replace the subconscious tapes in your mind with positive perceptions of the past. He can heal your subconscious mind by the power of the Holy Spirit and give you a true interpretation of events in your life.

Points To Remember

1. Sometimes the most difficult aspect of personality reconstruction is not the healing but the identification of the areas of your life that need to be healed.
2. Any healing requires time plus care and discipline.
3. Your present behavior, whether you are aware of it or not, is conditioned by memories buried in your innermost personality.
4. Jesus wants to replace the subconscious tapes in your mind with positive perceptions of the past.

Chapter 2

WHOLENESS: THE FIVE BUILDING BLOCKS

What is wholeness? *Wholeness* (not "wholistic"), from a Christian perspective, recognizes Christ as the cornerstone of spiritual riches. Jesus came so we might have life, and have it "more abundantly" (John 10:10). God's Word offers wisdom to deal with life's problems, providing the guidelines for successful, abundant living.

Wholeness, as defined in Mark 12:30-31, is the doorway to God's riches: "And thou shalt love the Lord thy God with all thy *heart,* and with all thy *soul,* and with all thy *mind,* and with all thy *strength:* This is the first commandment. And the second is like, namely this, Thou shalt love thy *neighbour* as thyself. There is none other commandment greater than these."

The heart represents your *spiritual* component. The mind and soul are the *mental* and *emotional* aspects of your personality. Strength is your *physical,* human frame. To love one's neighbor as your-

THE FIVE
BUILDING BLOCKS
OF WHOLENESS

SPIRITUAL (heart)	
MENTAL (mind)	**EMOTIONAL** (soul)
PHYSICAL (strength)	**SOCIAL** (neighbor)

self specifies the *social* need required to make you a whole individual.

These verses in Mark explain that God needs to see an expression of love in your life in three areas: Love for *God*. Love for *self*. Love for *others*.

Jesus was willing to die on the cross for you and me because of love. Once you see yourself as lovable by the Savior, you are better able to love yourself, others, and God.

If you truly love God with all your heart, soul, mind, and strength, then you have completely fulfilled all the requirements of the first half of the law. Mark 12:31 goes on to explain that if you love your neighbor the way you love and respect yourself, you have found the secret to a joyous, bountiful life.

There are five aspects of your character. Each of these areas affects the others and forms your complete personality. A weak or incomplete block can create personality problems or cause weaknesses in other areas. Let's discuss each building block separately.

1. Your Heart—The Spiritual Block

The heart is the spiritual dimension of man's being. By faith, your heart touches God and receives His life-giving Spirit. (See Romans 10:9-10.) If your heart is open, you can receive life that is eternal and overflowing with the fruit of God's Spirit. (See John 3:16; Galatians 5:22-23.) You can also develop a peaceful and positive attitude toward life. (See Philippians 4:6-8.)

To be in harmony with God's plan for your life, you

must learn to be dead to self and alive to Christ. God's plan begins to work in your life when you tear down the self-made castles over which you reign supreme. To have self at the center of your universe is a lonely experience. When things go wrong, your personal pride will not enable you to endure the demise of your kingdom. Hence, you are always living on egg shells, fearing one day your empire may crumble. Extreme anxiety and neurotic behavior can be linked to the throne room of your heart.

Is Christ on the throne of your heart? If He is, then all glory and responsibility is focused on Him. When God is reigning in your life, you are released from putting up pretenses or from wearing a mask. You can be yourself without the fear of being un-lovable.

When you learn to take your acceptance and approval from God, you have stability in your life. God is your foundation, and He will never fail you. People will always let you down because human love is fleeting. God's love, however, is bountiful and constant.

God's Word and love will set you free from the tyranny of your own kingdom. You'll submit to the higher power of God and free yourself from your own self-imposed prison. Make Christ Lord today, and you will be free to be yourself.

When you know God loves you, your heart is full of loving compassion for others. Hold love in your heart! Turn on the love button and make it part of your personality.

Releasing Spiritual Energy

Hebrews 11:6 says that you can never please God without faith—without depending on Him. With faith in your heart you no longer need to react negatively to circumstances. In times of trouble, you can remember that the problems you are experiencing will pass like all others before them.

Trust God, then you can operate with love and peace by praising Him for your blessings and past victories. Claim new victories for today. Resist the devil, and he will flee from you. Any problem you now face will disappear as a vapor, so don't give it emotional energy.

Keep your attention focused on things that are beautiful, pleasant, positive, and Christlike, then your heart will be at peace. Don't feed on or sow confusion and disharmony; for you will reap what you sow. Don't worry about anything; instead pray about everything. Tell God your needs, then thank Him for His answers. (See Philippians 4:6-7.) Keep the channel of your heart clear by holding an attitude of thankfulness and praise on your lips.

Hebrews 13:15 states, "Let us offer the sacrifice of praise to God continually, that is, the fruit of our lips giving thanks unto his name." Praising God is an act of the will. Learn to praise Him in every situation,then you'll experience freedom from this world's circumstances. Praising God releases spiritual energy and renounces the dominion of evil forces over our lives. Praise God right now in a loud voice and don't stop until you feel victory well up in your heart.

God's Kingdom rests in the heart of man!

2. & 3. Your Mind And Soul

The mental and emotional building blocks of your personality are your mind and soul. Your mind must be renewed to the image of God. "Be ye transformed by the renewing of your mind, that ye may prove what is that good and acceptable, and perfect will of God" (Romans 12:2).

In God's program of personality reconstruction, the predetermined beliefs of the mind affect your growth potential. A negative self-image can hinder God's spiritual flow through you. Your state of mind will determine the difference between success and failure, abundance or lack, joy or sadness.

The Bible states, "If thou canst believe, all things are possible to him that believeth" (Mark 9:23). Your mind is transformed through belief in God's Word. Reconstruction of your personality takes place when you accept this fact as truth. Read the Word of God and these truths will come alive.

Your thoughts are creative. Creative thoughts and imaginations operate by principles and laws that can be used for your good. Negative spiritual confessions hinder God's potential in you.

Creative thoughts need to be harnessed. Learn to direct and steer your thoughts as you would your automobile. Your thought-images will attract to your life what you believe is reality.

Controlling Your Thoughts

Every thought can either be a constructive prayer or a destructive prayer. When thoughts are infused with faith, you can become what you imagine. Whatever you allow to control your mind controls you. Whatever you impress upon your subconscious mind can take form in the material world.

Begin now to reset your thought pictures. Let your thought pictures be overflowing in God's blessing. Direct the images placed on the screen of your mind. The Bible says that as a man "thinketh in his heart, so is he" (Proverbs 23:7). Your imagined self-image affects your will, emotions, and actions, and as a result, determines your behavior.

Whatever you give attention to grows, magnifies, and multiplies in your experience. Focus your mind on God's abundance and whatever is lovely and good. Pray for blessing on others. They will prosper and so will you.

God's program for reconstruction of the personality rests upon the promise that no thing, person, situation, or condition is impossible or without hope.

Years ago, I was invited to attend the wedding of a close friend. Upon arriving at the rather dilapidated church building, I was met by the pastor. This man, in his late sixties, was bent over by the weight of his ministry. He lacked any expression of peace and joy, and I sensed a feeling of gloom surrounding his life. This dear brother lived in the basement of the church and walked with an unshakable heaviness.

As I entered the church, I saw a banner over the organ that gave a clue to what was taking place in the mind and heart of this pastor. The banner read, "God Loves An Impossible Mission."

Unfortunately, the impossibility was only in the mind and soul of this pastor. God's will is demonstrated in the spiritual truth that no situation is impossible.

Do you feel your life is impossible? Poverty is in the spirit and soul of the individual, but abundance also originates from within. Claim God's power to change your situation around by claiming this truth in Luke 1:37: "For with God nothing shall be impossible."

4. The Physical Building Block

The age in which we live is the most polluted, poisoned, and chemically saturated period of all time. It is impossible to avoid radiation, air and water pollution, chemicals in our food and clothing, and other harmful substances found in our environment.

Yet, in spite of these obstacles, Scripture admonishes us to take care of ourselves. "Your body is the temple of the Holy Ghost" (1 Corinthians 6:19,20).

When I was a boy, I believed I was indestructible. I watched Superman movies and dreamed I was made of steel. In my imagination I saw myself fighting crime, leaping from tall buildings, and aiding damsels in distress.

Throughout my years of school athletics, I held this invincible image of myself. It wasn't until I experienced a serious injury playing football that this concept about my physical strength changed.

Later, in college I learned how the body is made and how it functions. This created a new awareness and desire to take care of myself and not abuse the physical temple God had given me.

Health awareness establishes greater discipline in our lives. This doesn't mean we should all strive to become Atlas-like weight lifters, but we should eat correctly, get plenty of sleep, and exercise regularly. When you have a physical problem, see a health professional—a medical doctor, a chiropractic physician, dentist, etc.—one who is trained to identify and treat specific disorders.

The Bible teaches us to be good stewards of the gifts and talents God has given us. If you don't use your God-given physical attributes, you may lose them. After the age of forty, the effects of aging and gravity can cause a man's height to decrease one inch every ten years. In addition, a man's muscle mass may decrease 25-40[6] due to disuse and atrophy. As a result of decreased physical activity and muscular stimulation, bone density may actually demineralize, causing osteoporosis.

How are you developing God's gifts to you? Do you exercise and take care of your body?

Beyond The Symptoms

When dealing with physical problems, be solution oriented. Dig for the root cause to your problem before using drugs that simply treat the symptoms. Many physical ailments can be successfully cured with proper diet and supplements that strengthen your body and help you fight disease.

In my practice I follow this principle: natural first, drugs second, and surgery as the last resort.

Your attitudes and emotions can also affect the physical aspect of your personality. If you choose to be ruled by the negative emotions of hatred, anger, or self-pity, you will eventually reap the results in your body.

Your emotional state can affect your physical health. David wrote in Psalm 31, "My life is spent with grief, and my years with sighing: my strength faileth because of mine iniquity, and my bones are consumed" (verse 10). A heaviness of spirit can create psychosomatic or physical disease.

Love, forgiveness, and acceptance are the strongest healing agents available to you. If you can learn to love people, forgive your enemies, accept yourself and others, you can enjoy a life of peace and health.

5. The Social Building Block

You are a social being with responsibilities not only to yourself but to others. You cannot do your own thing without affecting others in some way.

No man is an island. A healthy, whole person realizes his need for social contact. You were created to love not only God but also yourself and others.

The hermit's life is not God's plan. People may seek God alone for a season, but God intends for us to establish healthy relationships with other people. A person who isolates himself from others and lives in a vacuum soon loses contact with reality.

Research has proven that people who have been isolated from others for long periods of time, or have undergone some form of sensory deprivation or monotony, enter bizarre states of delusion, hallucination, and paranoia. God expects us to love Him and others, finding healing through healthy relationships.

Life is more than being the king of your own castle. Healthy relationships are what *wholeness* is all about. You need other people. To refuse to build meaningful relationships, or to allow breakdown in relationships through unforgiveness, spells isolation and degeneration.

Broken relationships (friendships, marriages, etc.) cause chaos and confusion. The Bible says to keep your accounts short and not "let the sun go down on your wrath" (Ephesians 4:26). Any anger engendered in a personal relationship should never be dissipated by yelling or screaming. Instead, direct those energies toward solving the problem.

No person or situation has the power to manipulate you unless you unwittingly surrender to the problem. In a sense, you can inflict your own punishment. Always channel your energies to problem solving. Confront the situation in love and release it to God.

Going The Second Mile

In Jesus' day, it was the law that a Roman soldier could order a Jewish civilian to carry his gear a mile for him. The Jews saw this as a form of imposed slavery. It was a degrading experience that left the individual feeling used and humiliated. But Jesus told the Jews to offer to go a second mile. (See Matthew 5:41.)

Jesus shows us how to react positively to the circumstances of our lives by willfully choosing to help others—even our enemies. To be ordered to carry someone's load grudgingly against your will berates your spirit and makes you feel like a slave. However, under the same circumstances, if *you* decide to go the second mile, you come away from the experience with dignity. Look for opportunities to go the second mile with others—a husband, wife, or a boss. It will not only be good for them but good for you as well.

Strive to see the good in the other individual, to hunt for it, and to expect it. If you expect to see the good in life and others, invariably you'll find it.

As a Christian who is dead to sin, you can refuse to acknowledge the disparaging remarks of others as insults and taunts. Remember, as a "dead man" alive unto God, you should *act* with a right attitude to situations and not *react* to circumstances. Act as you know you should rather than as your old nature would have you do.

You can become a *whole* person, complete in Jesus Christ. (See Colossians 2:10.) As you yield each area of your personality to the Lord, you will become more and more the whole, complete, and mature person God created you to be.

Points To Remember

1. Wholeness is the doorway to God's riches.
2. Choose the truths of God that never change. Keep your attention focused on those things that are beautiful and Christlike.
3. Praise God in all circumstances. Your praise will release His power in your life.
4. Learn to direct and steer your thoughts as you would an automobile. Your thought images will often attract into your life that which is reality.
5. Be solution oriented when dealing with physical problems. Dig for the root cause.
6. Establish healthy relationships with other people, and you will experience wholeness in your life.

Chapter 3

GET TO THE ROOT OF THE PROBLEM

God the Creator wants to get to the root of your problems instead of simply treating the symptoms. Most treatments given by medical doctors and psychologists merely treat the symptoms of illnesses and do not get to the root cause. God is more thorough.

The root of man's problem is *sin*—and only God has the solution. You were born with the sinful, prideful nature of Adam. When God's love touches you and you respond positively to His touch, you shed Adam's nature and take on the new nature of Christ—one of humility and grace. This is the process of restoration and renewal.

Christ's humble nature is one of truth and peace. Isaiah talks about the peacefulness of the Christ-life: "And the work of righteousness shall be peace; and the effect of righteousness quietness and assurance for ever" (Isaiah 32:17).

You may have experienced darkness and inner turmoil in your life. The Holy Spirit wants to target those areas and work healing into your personality.

When God heals your memories, He brings peace, quietness, and a quality of assurance—forever.

Jesus is the tree of life, and that tree is rooted in humility. The fruit of that tree includes joyfulness, contentment, tenderness, self-control, pliability, and patience. (See Galatians 5:22-23.) These are the attributes you take on when God gives you a new nature in Christ. The apostle Paul put it succinctly: "Put on the new man, which is renewed in knowledge after the image of him that created him" (Colossians 3:10).

Your mind is renewed when you apply the truths found in God's Word. It's not magic—it's a learning process. As you reeducate and reprogram your old man with new information, a kind of "spiritual behavior modification" takes place.

The prophet Ezekiel speaks symbolically of Jesus as a river of life flowing through the desert, bringing life to everything it touches: "Then he said unto me, These waters issue out toward the east country, and go down into the desert, and go into deep sea: which being brought forth into the sea, the waters shall be healed. And it shall come to pass, that every thing that liveth, which moveth, whithersoever the rivers shall come, shall live" (Ezekiel 47:8-9).

Your life may be like a desert—empty of love, without fellowship, and spiritually dry. Jesus brings life to that kind of desert. There, He plants the tree of life, rooted in humility and watered with His river of love.

The "deep sea" described in this passage is indicative of your subconscious. Many of your experiences and memories have been so painful or unpleasant that you felt the only way to survive them was to submerge them deep into your subconscious. Yet they occasionally seep to the surface, creating new emotional problems.

When God brings these submerged memories to the surface, He exposes them to His love and forgiveness. Our pain and weaknesses are brought to the light so He can turn them into strength and joy.

Receiving God's Love

Some people believe they are too unworthy to receive any kind of love from God. They consider themselves too dirty to merit God's forgiveness and reconstruction. They live in senseless misery, often rationalizing this as their "cross" to bear in life. This attitude destroys their faith and limits their potential.

Many people get into the bondage of attempting to make themselves worthy for God. They fulfill every "jot and tittle" of the Bible—as they see it—going to sometimes bizzare extremes in pietistic legalism. They agonize through life trying to achieve religious perfection and striving to become worthy of God's gifts. Yet they are always aware of their unworthiness because of the past they drag around with them.

Many legalistic Christians are oppressed, obsessed, and depressed. They tend toward self-pity mixed with false self-righteousness. This is not what Christ offers us. We can never merit God's love and forgiveness through our own self-efforts.

Many Christians labor under the incorrect impression that if they fail to perform perfectly, God will take His gift of salvation away from them. But this is not God's way. God operates on grace—free grace. His way is in direct contrast to the fleshly, merit-type systems many of us set up for ourselves and use to judge others.

The apostle Paul came to the conclusion that there was no goodness in his own flesh. (See Romans 7:18-25.) Only by opening your spirit to the Holy Spirit can you live a Spirit-directed life and find increasing fulfillment and happiness.

Paul talked to the Galatians extensively about this: "I am crucified with Christ, nevertheless I live; yet not I, but Christ liveth in me: and the life which I now live in the flesh I live by the faith of the Son of God, who loved me, and gave himself for me" (Galatians 2:20).

Only God is perfect, and only through Him can you begin to move toward spiritual perfection. He isn't looking for you to be a "super Christian." He already accepts you as you are, and He asks you to do the same. Once you are established in His acceptance, you can move confidently toward the perfection He has fashioned for you.

Getting Rid Of Guilt

Prayer is your communication connection with God, and He wants to talk with you daily. God wants to express His love for you, but because of improper feelings of guilt and condemnation, you may often ignore His love.

It is important to pray even when you don't feel like it—when you don't feel worthy to come into God's presence. In fact, prayer is even more necessary at such times. This feeling of unworthiness is your conscience nudging you to seek God's forgiveness and mercy right now!

In 1 John 1:9, it is stated, "If we confess our sins, he is faithful and just to forgive us our sins, and to cleanse us from all unrighteousness." God loves you. He has forgiven you. Accept His forgiveness of your sins by faith.

Some Christians shake their fist at God about the past. They have not learned to confess resentment and bitterness as sin. They have yet to realize that God is not their adversary.

God is not "out to get you." Unpleasant situations come into your life to teach you how to cope, to give you opportunities for personal growth, and to lead you into dependence upon Him. When you come to the point of despair over your own efforts, your growth and maturation in God's grace will begin.

You may be experiencing guilt from the past which you haven't wholly confessed and asked the Lord to take from you. Whether this is true or false guilt, it can be very binding.

Ask the Lord to show you what is causing you to feel guilt. Then, see Jesus in that situation, forgiving you for the inadequacies you were demonstrating at that time. If you realize you've experienced false guilt, see Jesus changing your perception of the event. Imagine Him erasing the false guilt and healing your feelings of inadequacy.

Keys To Healing

The key to unlocking the chains of the personality is *giving* to others. This means responding to the needs of those around you, praying for others, sharing a meal, listening to someone who's hurting, or helping another with chores.

Helping others indicates your confidence in God's ability to help you. And it works! Giving of yourself develops a feeling of self-worth that helps you recognize the value of others. When you reach out to other people, it is easy to see Jesus reaching out to you. In order to receive, you must first give of yourself.

Sincere desire is another key element to healing. You must really want to be well. Many people actually enjoy their self-pity by feeding morbidly on grudges and stewing in their unhappy memories. They may talk as if they want their lives to be different, but in their hearts they want everything to remain just as it is.

Don't plot injury to yourself by dwelling in *self-pity*. Don't be a Silly Empty Little Fellow—Plotting Injury To Yourself.

To determine if self-pity may be standing in the way of your healing, ask yourself these questions:

Does your present personality make others feel guilty for not taking care of you? Does this kind of attention give you a sense of power over others? Is your illness or attitude your way of punishing your-self or your family?

Some people don't want to be physically and emotionally well because true health might:

*Destroy their power over people (manipulation).

*Force them to take charge of their life.

*Eliminate the concern and attention they attract from others.

*Magnify their present sense of guilt. They feel they need to be punished, and their illness meets that need, providing a temporary release of guilt feelings. If they get well, they will not have an outlet for their guilt.

Ask yourself, "Do I really want to be well? Do I really want success, victory, and health? Am I 45% in favor of getting better but 55% in favor of being sick?" That small percentage of difference can hold back your release and growth.

You must want to change more than you want to stay the same. Take the *risk!* Be Rich In Spiritual Knowledge by not accepting illness as an answer to your problems.

You can't solve all of your problems on your own. Trying to change your life by your own efforts is a waste of time. You can find yourself only by letting go of yourself. Learn to look to God's Word and deal with your problems scripturally.

Give God Time

Many people begin their process of personality

reconstruction and give up when the cure isn't "instant." No healing takes place overnight. A cut on your finger happens in a moment but heals over weeks. A cut on your memory happens in minutes; but after it has festered, the healing may take months.

When Nehemiah rebuilt the wall of Jerusalem, he refused to be distracted from the task before him. In the same way, you must not come down from the wall until the job is finished. Keep at it until you're completely renewed. Close out your mind to negative distractions!

Satan, in the continuing war for your mind, will attack your life. He will try to ruin the new-found hope, healing, and confidence you are experiencing in Christ. His influence is subtle. It comes at you through the media, friends, situations, and even well-meaning but immature, Christian brothers and sisters.

After having a bad cold or the flu, you try to maintain your health through discipline and extra care of your body. The same principle holds true for emotional and spiritual healing. After healing there is a recovery period that requires extra care of your spirit. When you ask God to begin the healing process, He does. But it is your responsibility to take the proper medication and trust Him to complete what He has begun.

As you persevere with prayer and patience, God brings continuous, gradual healing. I often tell people to "soak in prayer"—the way you would soak an injured ankle or swab a cut with antiseptic.

Reconstruction of the personality isn't a one-time fix. It is a day-by-day living in His grace, mercy, and love.

Identifying The Giants In Your Life

God promised the land of Canaan as the inheritance of the children of Israel. When Moses was approaching the Promised Land, he sent spies ahead to gather "intelligence" about the land and its people. The spies returned shaking with fear at the giants they had seen. (See Numbers 13:27-33.)

The people, after listening to the spies' reports, felt that God had failed them. Their faith crumbled, and they decided they weren't going to be successful in their occupation of the Promised Land. The spies' faithless and distorted misrepresentation of reality taught the Israelites to fear.

Your past failures, embarrassments, and hurts may have distorted your present reality, creating an unnecessary sense of fear and dread. God has an inheritance for you, just as He did for the Israelites. The benefits of His Kingdom are yours if you will reach out and take them. But fear can stop you dead in your tracks, making it impossible for you to receive all God has for you. Don't allow your past to condemn your present and your future.

Normal fear is healthy and helps you avoid danger. Abnormal fear, however, can be destructive to your personality. This kind of fear is learned. To fear something persistently causes a sense of panic and terror that results in abnormal phobias, obsessions, and complexes.

God's reconstruction of the personality begins with tearing down the false and debilitating limits of binding fear. Once this is done, your true Spirit-filled potential will be set free, and you can claim your rightful inheritance in the Father's Kingdom.

The Fear Teacher

The most successful teacher of fear is Satan himself. Satan is a con-artist—the great deceiver. He is especially clever at convincing people that they can't cope. By programming you to accept certain false limitations about yourself and your potential, Satan builds fear into your system. He dupes you into believing the worst about yourself and makes you think your shortcomings represent all you can ever be.

I once worked for a man who had a charming but very intimidating personality. It seemed he could get people to do anything he wished. When he dealt with me, I often felt the pressure of his subtle manipulation.

He could point his finger at an adversary and shout, "You're through in this town!" His words put fear into the hearts of everyone within earshot because they believed his prediction would come true. His authoritative manner was devastating.

Since I was having difficulty dealing with this man, I began to pray about the situation. The Lord showed me that the man had no substance. His words were threatening but empty. As I considered his past threats, I realized he had never come through on a single one of them. Although many people were intimidated by him and afraid of him, he was nothing more than a roaring, toothless lion.

This is similar to what happened to the Israelites. They believed the words of faithless frauds. They ignored the promises of God and accepted the fear-filled words of spies who had lost heart. The result was forty years of needless wandering in the wilderness.

This is also what happens to people who have become unconsciously programmed by fear. Over the years, they have surrendered their thoughts to destructive ideas.

Our dog, Ebony, is a Rottweiler—an aggressive and powerful breed of guard dog. Generally, these dogs are fearless, but Ebony was not typical of her famous ancestors.

While cleaning the house one day, my wife noticed that Ebony was terrified of the vacuum cleaner. Later, when the dog would go into one of her hyperactive fits, my wife would tie Ebony to the silent vacuum cleaner. Immediately, this frantic puppy would become lifeless and sit looking helplessly at the terrible, electric monster.

One evening I was resting on the bed upstairs when I heard a loud commotion. It sounded like a tornado roaring through the house, destroying everything in its path. Glass was breaking and pots were falling on the floor. I jumped from the bed and ran to the top of the stairs, shouting, "Stop! Stop!"

Ebony, with tail tucked between her legs, was tearing around the house being chased by the vacuum cleaner. I frantically tried to calm her down, alleviate her fears, and reason with her. But how do you explain to a dog that the monster she is running from has no power unless she pulls it?

We, as intelligent human beings, sometimes react in the same foolish way. We energize fears or ideas that have no power in and of themselves. Our heavenly Father wants to alleviate our unfounded anxieties and teach us to trust in Him. God wants us to live above our irrational emotions and take authority over them. He is shouting, "Stop!" to the destructive cycle of fear.

You are a child of God with a divine inheritance. The battle has already been fought, and the victory has been won. But you must believe in the victory. You must claim it for yourself and make it your personal victory—even when it appears that disaster is looming just ahead. You must realize that fear can be cast aside. Every "disaster" is just another ploy—a trick to rob you of your divine inheritance. It is a trick of Satan's to confuse you and distract you from God's promise.

Satan seeks to convince us that we are the only ones going through trials. He tells us that no one else has ever been where we are—no one else has failed as we have failed, and no one else is as weak as we are. Satan wants us to think that our situation is so unique that Christ's healing and forgiveness can't reach us.

No matter how new or contemporary your problem seems, Jesus knows each crisis is just more of the same—a tempering of your faith. No situation is so new that God can't heal and forgive through the blood of Jesus Christ.

Paralyzed Potential

Satan works on your life with his arsenal of weapons: fear, doubt, anger, hostility, worry, false guilt, and condemnation.

With these weapons, he has paralyzed the lives of many people. Satan thrills at stifling your creative potential and limiting your service to others. He delights in seeing you hide the talents God has given you.

One of the hardest rebukes Jesus gave was to the servant who hid his talent and did not develop it. This man was paralyzed by fear, and his potential and privileges in God's Kingdom were lost. (See Matthew 25:14-30.)

Get in touch with who you are and what your gifts are. Let God show you your talents. Let Him show you your potential for development. Are you loving? Can you teach or entertain? Do you have a ministry of service to others?

Many people look at others around them and play the deadly game of comparison. They think other people have more talent or ability than they have.

The result of such thinking is bitterness toward others and a belittling of one's self. We must guard against the habit of comparison. In the eyes of Jesus, each of us is valuable in our own right and no worse or better than anyone else.

A poor self-image not only paralyzes our talents but also our relationships. A person who has a low self-esteem becomes more and more *emotionally isolated*. He is always on guard and feels he's the victim of constant, unjustified personal attack. He thinks he must keep his distance in order to survive, creating an *attitude of independence* that says, "I don't need anyone."

People who have such an attitude assume that everyone dislikes them. They expect to be rejected. The sad thing is that what they believe in their minds becomes reality in their lives. Their negative and suspicious approach to life repels other people and damages their personal relationships. Satan has paralyzed their potential for an abundant life of healthy emotions and rewarding endeavors.

Our personalities need to be reconstructed so our defeated self-image does not paralyze our dreams. The Bible states that "where there is no vision the people perish" (Proverbs 29:18). As a man dreams in his heart so is he. We don't live *in* our dreams or *on* our dreams, but we must live *by* our dreams.

God's plan for personality reconstruction is to put the big dream and vision back within your heart. Attempt great things for God and then wait for Him to orchestrate answers to your visions and dreams.

Your dream mechanism and creative imagination were given by God. If you employ them properly, they can be used as a vehicle for wholeness.

The Fear Process

The progression to fearful living is simple yet alarming. You open your mind to a fearful thought, and the mind directs it into your heart where it is emotionalized. Then the thought, which has become an emotion, is expressed, and you verbalize it. The emotionalized thought becomes an overpowering "fact."

Many Christians are snagged by their negative confessions: "Oh Lord, I'm no good," they whine. "I can't do any work for you." Or, "I'll never be well." Or, "God just doesn't love me like He loves others." And so on. They confess their own self-directed limitations and are condemned by their words. Through the verbalization of their fears, they begin to mold their character.

People who have become paralyzed by fear exhibit certain characteristics in their personalities. Fearful people are often frozen in *indecision*. They have mentally retired from life and can't seem to budge from their lethargy. A fear of failure or danger keeps them from making commitments or striving for achievement. They tend to spiritualize their indecision until all opportunities have vanished. Instead of learning from their past mistakes and failures, they become so *overcautious* that they are unable to enjoy even the simplest ventures in life.

This kind of fearful living leads to *procrastination* and avoidance of any new challenges in life. People paralyzed by fear use excuses and alibis to forestall victory, success, and fulfillment.

The mind determines what is in your heart, so guard your mind carefully. If you let negativism slip through your mind into your heart, eventually it will come out of your mouth.

Jesus made it very clear that we will be judged on the basis of what comes out of our hearts: "A good man out of the good treasure of the heart bringeth forth good things: and an evil man out of the evil treasure bringeth forth evil things. But I say unto you, That every idle word that men shall speak, they shall give account thereof in the day of judgment. For by thy words thou shalt be justified, and by thy words thou shalt be condemned" (Matthew 12:35-37).

Our words are extensions of our emotions, and our emotions are extensions of our thoughts. Learn to discipline your thought process and you will prevent thoughts from becoming emotionalized. Analyze your fears and defuse irrational thoughts with God's Word. Let faith stand guard at the door of your mind to keep destructive thoughts and words from running free. This will prevent the ugly process of spiritual and emotional degeneration.

Defusing Fear

Before you can deal with your anxieties and fears,

you must first know what they are. The following exercises will help you determine your fears and what causes them.

1. Study your feelings of fear for one week and make a list of them. Try to determine what circumstances precede the arousal of these fears in your heart.

2. Try to pinpoint the time of your fear's greatest arousal. A fear of doctors for example may actually be a symptom of fear of authority, death, or pain.

3. Construct a fear hierarchy. List your fears and give each one a rating from zero to ten.

4. Jot down one or two statements from the Bible as a positive response to each fear. Have Scripture ready to keep that fear from entering your heart.

For example, Bob has a fear of cats. He thinks, "I see the cat across the road. The cat seems docile. People near the cat are calm. Why shouldn't I feel the same? 'I can do all things through Christ.' I'll keep relaxed as I approach."

5. If you have an abnormal fear or hurt of any kind—perhaps one that people would call a "little" fear, such as fear of dogs, fear of elevators, or an inability to talk about death—ask God to show you the origin of that fear. What created it? Where and when was that seed of fear planted? Ask the Lord to give you insight into your past.

6. When the origin of that fear is brought to your mind, visualize Jesus in that past situation. Ask Him to relive the situation with you, to go back with you to that moment, and to take away the fear or hurt

you've come to associate with it. Ask for the key that will release the pain of the past and replace it with God's peace.

7. Visualize yourself going through that past situation victoriously and living victoriously in the present. For example, if you have a fear of speaking in public, imagine yourself today speaking calmly and effectively to a crowd—with Jesus right there beside you. If you have a fear of dogs, visualize yourself petting and playing with a large dog—with Jesus right there with you. Remember the Scripture verse that God has given you for every situation: "I can do all things through Christ which strengtheneth me" (Philippians 4:13).

The giants in your life are not beyond the healing power of God. The first step toward healing, however, is identifying the giants that may be hindering your potential for God's Kingdom and keeping you from your rightful inheritance as God's child.

Allow the Lord to help you identify the giants of fear in your life and release them to Him. Jesus will defuse the force behind your fears and replace them with His perfect peace.

Points To Remember

1. Only God is perfect, and only through Him can you begin to move toward spiritual perfection.
2. God loves you. He has forgiven you. He wants to use you mightily in His Kingdom.

3. Pray daily. Prayer is your communication connection with God.
4. You must sincerely desire to be well. Let self-pity, guilt, and unhappy memories go.
5. Persevere. No healing takes place overnight. Live day-by-day, in His grace, mercy, and love.
6. Destructive fear is learned. The most successful teacher of fear is Satan himself.
7. You are a child of God with a divine inheritance. The battle has already been fought, and the victory has been won. But *you* must believe in the victory.
8. Your personality needs to be reconstructed so your defeated self-image does not paralyze your dreams.
9. The mind determines what is in your heart, so guard your mind carefully. If you let negativism slip through your mind into your heart, eventually it will come out of your mouth.
10. Jesus will replace the giants of fear in your life with His perfect peace.

Chapter 4

BREAKING WITH THE PAST

Forgiveness is a necessary part of the process of reconstruction. Unforgiveness will block your prayers; refusing to forgive refuses you access to healing. You cannot blame others for any of your problems. It does not matter what kind of experiences you have gone through, what has happened in your family's history, or what bad deals you've been forced to take.

When this life is at an end, it will be only you and God, face to face. Your parents, no matter how much damage they may have done, will not be there for you to blame. You won't be able to point at anyone and say, "If it weren't for them, I would have done better." You will finally have to take responsibility for yourself. If you don't do it now, there won't be any avoiding it then.

Responsibility is really *response-ability*. You must have the ability to respond to God's love—and you can't have that ability until you give up all grudges and bitterness toward others. If you cling to your past, you become a "woe is me" individual. You must realize that you are a big part of the problem and have only yourself to blame.

Our relationship with God is essentially a product of His active forgiveness. It is not based on our inherent goodness. Therefore, my constructive relationship with others should also be based on my forgiveness, rather than on their goodness. Unforgiveness is a very destructive attitude that will cause physical and emotional disease. (See Proverbs 14:30.) God will not forgive you if you don't forgive others. (See Mark 11:26.)

It's impossible to receive reconstruction of your personality if you retain unforgiveness in your heart.

Painful Memories

Forgiveness was the key to Tom's personality reconstruction. He writes: "I've had to seek healing for memories over time. They've come up in situations where relationships were threatened or problems created—all because of something from my past."

Tom had suffered from a long series of hurting memories. Certain ones occurred over and over and plagued him daily. They had become as much a part of him as breathing. Satan used these memories to keep him divided from God and from others.

One experience had hurt him deeply for years, causing Tom tremendous fear and insecurity. It involved a breakdown in a relationship between another person and himself. It really wasn't that big a deal to begin with, but over the years it had taken on mammoth proportions. The pain of the memory beat against him daily, and each night Tom went to bed emotionally exhausted.

Finally, one day, he prayed, "Okay, Jesus, you come into this problem. Tear down the wall I've built between myself and this other person."

The Lord responded to this prayer, and Tom could see the Lord loving both himself and the other person. As this hurt was exposed, he cried because the pain was so great. Then Tom prayed for forgiveness for himself and the other person. He prayed, "Lord, take the harshness from this memory and don't allow it to hurt me anymore, please." Then he promised to ask forgiveness each time resentment tried to creep in.

Tom didn't really believe that a thorough healing was possible because this memory had been his constant companion for many years. But in faith he shut the emotional door on it the moment he prayed.

Several days later something clearly pointed back to that memory and the resentment he had harbored for so long. Tom stopped and thought, "What was it that hurt me? What was it?" He couldn't remember why that memory had caused so much anguish. To this day, the pain of that incident has been completely wiped away from Tom's mind.

In the days that followed that incident, Tom sat alone with the Lord many times and asked Him to walk with him back through various periods of his life. He asked the Lord to bring to his memory the hurts and fears that needed healing. Then he asked Jesus to heal them.

Tom discovered he had many resentments and grudges that needed healing. The Lord unveiled fears and hurts that had caused him problems without his realizing it. But God was faithful. He healed the innermost part of Tom's personality.

Forgiveness And Obedience

You must learn to respond to hurts and attacks from others with love. The person whose life is full of love needs no counseling because love conquers all. Is somebody hurting you? Try loving them in return.

Love, described in 1 Corinthians 13, begins with obedience. Love doesn't depend on feelings, and it doesn't rely on desire. Love involves obedience. The feelings will come later as your emotions are reprogrammed. God will not give you the feeling of love and joy of obedience until you have been obedient. He will keep urging you to step out in faith.

Forgiveness is an act of obedience that must be performed whether you feel like it or not. Forgiving others brings the joy of knowing that Jesus is pleased with your obedience. Then, your perception of others begins to change. The old ego, the old self, isn't keeping you dissatisfied, angry, or jealous anymore. The new man in you is identifying with Christ, loving those who hurt you, and learning how to deal with rejection.

What happens to all the hurt and irritation and bitterness? It's healed. The sting of pain can't remain once love is there and obedience is in operation. Obedience and forgiveness replace bitterness.

Once you start praying for others—especially for someone who has problems similar to yours—you'll find yourself being healed of your problems. Why? Because you are being obedient in love. Healing comes from love, and love comes from obedience. When you love, whether the person deserves it or not, whether you feel like it or not, whether you see the fruits of repentance in them or not—that's when healing occurs in your life.

Jesus never instructed us to keep a "black list" on the repentance records of others. We are to forgive others the same way we desire to be forgiven when we have failed time after time. We are to take every insult and every injury and sweeten it with God's love and our love—not with anger or self-pity.

Christ summed up the entire law in two commandments: Love God with your whole heart, and love your neighbor as yourself. What does He mean by loving your neighbor as yourself? You must learn to give to others in the same way you give to yourself. You provide for your own survival, your own nourishment, and your own comfort. Jesus said you must do the same for those around you by giving to others first before you take your share.

Keep on loving. Obedience must be continuous, so love must be continuous. Love is a relationship conditioned by responsible obedience to God's commandments. As you obey God and love Him and others, you experience a clear conscience and a sense of satisfaction that results in a healthy personality.

How To Forgive

Forgiveness is an act of the will. Envision the needs of the individual who has hurt you. Thank God for that person. Ask God to show you the good that has come out of the relationship. Ask God, by His Holy Spirit, to give you the ability to express love for the one you need to forgive.

The essence of forgiveness is not related to faith or feelings. Grant forgiveness to those who have harmed you whether you feel like it or not. This is not hypocritical; for as you release the other individual, God will release you. As you act out of obedience, God will flood your soul with love for the other person. (See Romans 5:5.)

Jesus looked down from the cross and said, "Father, forgive them; for they know not what they do" (Luke 23:34). Picture yourself looking down on your enemy and saying this prayer:

I release _____ (say person's name) from having to answer for the wrong he's done to me. Jesus, I ask you to forgive _____ for his insensitivity to me and my needs. Father, right now for-

give me for harboring negative and destructive thoughts about myself and others. Whenever this feeling of resentment or irritation surfaces, I will claim that God's love fills my soul. Relax my tension, and give me peace. I inhale your peace and exhale your love. Father, forgive _____ once and for all, for he does not know what he's done.

Erase the past with this prayer of forgiveness. Never dwell on old grievances or grudges—put them out of your mind. Come to a decision, forget the past, and fill your mind with love, peace, and hope. God's love can dissolve grudges.

Bottled-up emotion repressed into the innermost part of the personality needs God's release. Resentment and hostility are mental poisons that rob you of vitality, enthusiasm, and energy. Remember this scripture: "This one thing I do, forgetting those things which are behind, and reaching forth unto those things which are before. I press toward the mark" (Philippians 3:13-14).

Breaking The Hereditary Line

When an artistic masterpiece—a painting or piece of sculpture—has been marred or has deteriorated over time, restoration is necessary. Professionals spend long hours, and often years, restoring priceless art works and meticulously laboring over each minute detail. Extreme care must be taken to bring the work back to its original state.

The psalmist described a similar process of restoration in Psalm 23 when he said of the Lord, "He restoreth my soul." God is restoring you to the completeness of what He created you to be—a whole person, one with Him.

Restoration begins with cleansing. By the blood of Jesus Christ we are cleansed from sin. Once the cleansing has been accomplished, the restoration and renewal can begin. Many Christians accept Christ in a moment of salvation, but they fail to get renewed. This is like dusting off a great masterpiece without bothering to restore it to its original grandeur.

No great painting or sculpture was ever restored in a single day. Restoration by its very nature takes time. Don't get discouraged if it isn't happening as fast as you would like it to happen. God is a precise and loving craftsman, working carefully to heal the scars from your past.

What part of your personality needs God's reconstruction? You are body, soul, and spirit. The body, of course, is the physical. The spirit is the heart of you that operates in the unseen spiritual dimension. The soul, or your mind, is your *will,* your *emotions*, and your *intellect*. The healing power of God is usually most needed in these areas of the mind.

This is why Scripture speaks of our minds being *renewed*. The restored mind is the key to the transformed life. Transformation or reconstruction doesn't happen by accident. It comes through the direct work of God.

Romans 12:1-2 expresses it succinctly: "I beseech you therefore, brethren, by the mercies of God, that ye present your bodies a living sacrifice, holy, acceptable unto God, which is your reasonable service. And be not conformed to this world: but be ye transformed by the renewing of your mind, that ye may prove what is that good, and acceptable, and perfect, will of God."

You And Your Heredity

Two factors influence your personality: your *environment* and your *heredity.* You are more inclined to conform to your environment than to challenge it. Even when you intend to do otherwise, even when you determine to stand up to it, you often conform before you realize it.

The other influence on your life is your heredity. This is a tougher area to exert change in because, unlike your environment, your heredity is predetermined by history.

Heredity involves your biological makeup—all the physical attributes passed along from generation to generation through chromosomes. Your biological parents and grandparents (and other ancestors) have passed along a combination of physical characteristics to you.

They also have passed along some mental and emotional traits. Much of your personality is determined in the first few years of your life, when you are essentially a captive in your parents' home. Your heredity includes the attitudes, values, and emotional directives you received from your parents during these early, impressionable years.

A friend of mine was born into a poor family. His parents believed and practiced the philosophy that you must be poor to be godly. My friend still practices that philosophy. It's part of his hereditary line. It wasn't transmitted chemically at the moment of his conception, but it was transmitted undeniably through his parents in his most impressionable years.

Some people have both good hereditary lines and good environments. Others have good hereditary lines but bad environments, or weak hereditary lines with good environments.

The power of God can affect the hereditary line and strengthen you to deal with your environment. God also has the power to change your personality and, when necessary, break the hereditary line.

A Powerful Force

I counseled with a woman in her thirties who had lived a good Christian life, but she had been suffering emotionally for years. As I prayed with her for personality reconstruction, we asked the Lord to take her back as far as necessary—even three or four generations—on her mother's side first, then on her father's side. I found that this approach sometimes helps a person to better understand why they react to certain stimuli the way they do.

As we went back through the girl's hereditary line

on her mother's side, the Lord revealed to us physical disorders which were threatening the girl genetically. We claimed the power of Jesus' blood over them.

Then, as we went back through the father's side, the Lord spoke to me in my spirit and said, "Murder." I couldn't understand the incident in detail, but I had the overwhelming feeling that it was something horrible.

I thought it was just my vain imagination trying to make up something sensational, so I didn't verbalize what I felt. I kept praying with the girl and thumbing through the Scriptures, asking God to confirm the message in His Word. As I looked down at the page, I saw a phrase: " . . . murder in the streets."

Still, I was not convinced, so I asked the Lord to confirm further. The girl and I continued to pray together, through her conception, through her birth, and into her childhood. Suddenly, the girl stopped praying and looked at me.

"Has the Lord shown you anything about my mother trying to murder me?" she asked.

"No," I replied, because that wasn't what I had seen. I had no impulse involving both of her parents. Only her father. But she, too, had gotten the impression of murder.

"You know, it's strange," she began, "but ever since I was a little girl I've had terrifying nightmares in which I'm being strangled. And each time, I wake up unable to breathe, feeling as if someone were clutching my throat. It's as if a spirit of 'murder' were after me.

"But when I'm not dreaming," she continued, "I have a dreadful feeling of being attacked. I've often wondered if my parents had tried to smother me when I was a baby, or if someone else had."

I explained what I had seen in my spirit, and said, "But we have no proof."

The girl began to cry and pray. "God, I want to know the truth." She prayed, humbled herself before the Lord, and even though the details were unclear, she accepted her healing in faith. She was beautifully delivered from her torment that night.

Months later, I met the girl again. She told me that after a two-year absence, her sister had come to visit her recently. Her sister had been researching the family history and had discovered a distant relative on their father's side who had killed his wife and children and then committed suicide.

Everything became clear. The girl's sensitive soul had picked up on the spirit of murder that was being carried through the hereditary line to each generation.

I've found this same phenomenon at work in other people whose grandparents have practiced spiritism, used ouija boards, and so on. They often find themselves restless or troubled, angry or bitter. Only through deliverance and healing of the memories by the Holy Spirit can they find complete peace.

A New Hereditary Line

The reconstruction that God brings about in a person's life is all encompassing. It's thorough, radical regeneration—a true starting over. The Word of God says we become "new creatures" in Christ Jesus (2 Corinthians 5:17). A new creature does not need to endure the emotional-spiritual hereditary weaknesses of his parents or ancestors.

The hereditary line does not necessarily manifest itself in a single characteristic or set of characteristics. Most people have bits and pieces of both their parents and all four grandparents, as well as fragments of other long-gone relatives.

You may be carrying around some of the weaker emotional-spiritual traits of your predecessors and believe that you are stuck with them. Not so! Such an attitude denies the omnipotence of God. He can take your weaknesses and turn them into strengths. The Lord can also further strengthen your best traits. That's what regeneration is all about.

A study was made of two men: one a criminal and the other a minister. Both of their family histories were investigated in great detail, and the findings were overwhelming. The criminal came from a long line of criminals, and the minister came from a long line of solid, civic-minded Christians.

Each generation is responsible for either continuing or changing the pattern of its ancestry—either fulfilling or breaking its heritage. God is in the business of breaking the ungodly hereditary line and establishing a new godly one in its place. The work can begin in you, and it can continue in your children's children.

The process of breaking with the past begins with the Word of God. The Word of God renews the mind. The renewed mind yields a transformed life. The transformed life is completely different from the old life. It operates in the Spirit instead of the flesh and passes on spiritual truth to future generations.

This new hereditary line is described in Isaiah 59:12: "As for me, this is my covenant with them, saith the Lord; My spirit that is upon thee, and my words which I have put in thy mouth, shall not depart out of thy mouth, nor out of the mouth of thy seed, nor out of the mouth of thy seed's seed, saith the Lord, from henceforth and for ever."

The following is a renunciation and affirmation prayer to break sin's hereditary line in the life of born-again believers.

In the name of the Lord Jesus, I praise my heavenly Father for the eternal life He has given me. As God's own, purchased by the blood of the Lord Jesus Christ, I renounce all sins of my blood ancestors. I cancel out in Jesus' name all demonic working passed on to me by them. I claim the blood of Jesus and the work of the Holy Spirit. By His power, I take authority over Satan and all the powers of darkness in my life, renouncing the darkness and accepting the light of truth. I pull down all blindness which would hinder my under-standing.

As a servant and priest of God, I claim back all ground given to Satan by my ancestors, through the victory achieved by the Lord Jesus Christ in His redemptive work on the cross. By Jesus' blood and in His name, I curse all roots of bondage passed down to me. I claim the inheritance promised me in Romans 8:15-17 and Galatians 3:9-29 as an heir according to the promises given to God's seed. I sur-render myself wholly and completely to the Holy Spirit, and where the Spirit of the Lord is, there is liberty. Whom the Lord sets free is free indeed. Amen!

Name _____

Date _____

Points To Remember

1. Unforgiveness is a destructive attitude that will cause physical and emotional disease.
2. The person whose life is full of love needs no counseling because love conquers all.
3. Forgiveness is an act of obedience that must be performed whether you feel like it or not.
4. Forgiveness is an act of the will.
5. Resentment and hostility are mental poisons that rob you of vitality, enthusiasm, and energy.
6. Your mind is your will, emotions, and intel-

lect. This is where the healing power of God is usually most needed. The restored mind is the key to the transformed life.

7. Your biological parents and grandparents (and other ancestors) have passed along a full complement of physical characteristics to you.

8. The process of breaking with the past and breaking with an ungodly hereditary line begins with the Word of God. The Word of God renews the mind. The renewed mind yields a transformed life.

9. The transformed life is completely different from the old life. The new life operates in the Spirit instead of the flesh. It passes on spiritual truth to future generations, and a new hereditary line can be established.

Chapter 5

PERSONALITY RECONSTRUCTION THROUGH INNER HEALING

While reading this book, you may have become aware of certain areas of your life that need reconstructing. Before reconstruction can take place, however, healing must occur within your inner personality. This chapter will show you how to allow the Lord to heal those inner hurts of the past that are affecting your behavior in the present.

When praying for inner healing, you are doing a series of things. *First,* you are asking God to reveal all of your repressed memories. You are seeking to expose the darkest, most painful corners of your subconscious and the past it contains. It is in the dark recesses of your subconscious mind that your healing needs to happen. This exposure helps bring about healing.

Second, in your mind you are playing back your past—like looking at a movie frame by frame. As a memory comes up that needs spiritual attention, you "freeze" that frame and apply healing to that memory. You allow Christ to rearrange the scene and take away the pain and bitterness associated with that event.

Third, as these events come to your mind, you are sincerely forgiving any other person involved. You are voiding any blame you have placed on them. You are letting go of all pent-up hostilities and anger. You are also praying for your own forgiveness, asking the Lord to forgive you for not forgiving them sooner.

Finally, you are accepting the Lord's healing as He touches each painful circumstance. You are allowing the Lord to redeem your memory as He has already redeemed your past. You are accepting the blessing of His mercy and grace, freeing yourself from the tryanny of past memories. You can then walk in the fullness of the present.

A Checklist For Prayer

It is important to consider your past in as much detail as you can. To help you accomplish this, I'm providing a brief chronological checklist of possible situations that may need healing in your life. This list is in no way complete. As you read through it, other items will come to your mind. Write them down also and add them to the list. Expand the list as much as necessary, or cross off those items which do not apply to you.

Since your praying will take place over a period of time, you may want to write the date beside each item as you pray and receive healing for it.

Conception/Birth

*Parents weren't married
*Your mother was raped
*Pregnancy was accidental, not planned
*You have congenital physical problems
*Childbirth was traumatic
*An injury was suffered at birth
*You are the product of a failed abortion
*_____
*_____
*_____
*_____
*_____

Childhood/Teen Years

*You were abused as a child
*You were a victim of incest
*Your parents were negligent
*A parent was an alcoholic or drug user
*Your family was poor
*Your father beat your mother
*You were shy and clumsy
*You endured embarrassing physical problems
*You were forced or seduced into illicit sex
*Physical problems were misdiagnosed
*You were ridiculed because of your appearance
*Your parents divorced
*The parent who had custody of you remarried

*You were aware of your parents' infidelities
*You were discriminated against
*You had academic problems in school
* _____
* _____
* _____
* _____
* _____

Adulthood

*You were fired from your job
*You've been unable to find rewarding work
*You are afraid of failure
*You are afraid of success
*Your spouse has been unfaithful
*You have been unfaithful
*You have emotional problems
*You have suffered financial setbacks
*You have abused your children
*You are a victim of rape or abuse
*You are addicted to drugs or alcohol
*You made a misjudgment in business
*A friend has unjustly turned against you
*You have difficulty relating to people
*You're embarrassed because you are single
*You're afraid of marriage
*You're afraid of not being married
* _____
* _____
* _____

74

Praying For Healing Of Memories

I am going to outline a prayer for personality reconstruction as a model for you to follow. This is a prayer that will allow the Lord to heal your innermost thoughts and painful memories.

There are several parts to this prayer, covering different stages of your development. You should pray each section separately, allowing time for the Lord to minister to you. Ask God to lead you back through your entire past, step by step, and heal the memories that have been suppressed for so long.

I'm giving this prayer to you on paper, just as I have given it to many on tape, for several reasons. First, I cannot be with you personally at this moment.

Second, I want you to have access to this prayer at all times, whenever you feel you need it. I want you to be able to come back to this prayer over and over again, every time you feel encircled by doubts. Each time you pray through this prayer, you conquer any remaining shred of doubt, deceit, and unbelief.

Before praying this prayer for inner healing, you need to get prepared. Find a place where you can be completely relaxed and at ease. Close out all distractions—the TV, the radio, and even unplug the telephone. Draw the drapes, too. Close yourself in, alone with the Lord.

Take a few deep breaths and exhale slowly. Close your eyes and imagine all the tension leaving your body and mind. Slow down, become quiet, and center your thoughts on the Lord and the process of healing. Now you are ready to begin working through prayer.

A Prayer Of Surrender

Begin with this prayer of confession and confirmation. Invite the Spirit to begin the process of preparing you for healing as you pray this prayer of surrender.

Father, I realize I am unworthy, a sinner saved only by your grace. And for that I am grateful. Thank you, Jesus, for cleansing me of sin and accepting me into your life. Thank you for coming into my heart.

I confess my sins. Forgive me for not being as honest as I should; for not reading your Word as often as I should; for not being as loving as I should be. Forgive my weaknesses and my inconsistencies. Strengthen me through your Spirit. Teach me to walk more carefully in the Spirit and not in the flesh. Keep my heart open to your voice and leading.

Free me now from any bitterness or malice I'm feeling toward others. Forgive those who have hurt me, and forgive me for hurting others. Thank you for your healing forgiveness.

In the name of Jesus, I renounce all works of the Enemy in my life, and I unleash the power of the

Holy Spirit to work in me. I surrender everything to you, Lord, and ask you to be with me as I seek inner healing. I want your healing, and I long to be free from past failures and pain. I want to be rid of senseless and debilitating anxieties and fears.

Thank you, Father, for hearing my prayer and for being with me. Thank you for offering healing and peace in spite of my unworthiness. Thank you for being there when I need you. Amen.

Jesus is love and light. He can redeem the most unpleasant memories in the same way He forgives your past sins. Ask Him to give you the measure of faith you need to believe you'll be set free. Thank Him in advance for the miracle He is about to perform in your life right now.

As you read through this model prayer, allow Him to come in and begin to reprogram your subconscious "tapes." Perhaps, you will want to tape-record yourself as you pray this prayer out loud; then later, you can replay it to reaffirm your healing.

Fearfully And Wonderfully Made

You are ready to let the healing process begin. Visualize in your mind you and Jesus, standing side by side holding hands. Imagine yourself walking with Jesus back through your memories to the place and time of your birth. Allow the Spirit to guide your visualization. Follow the Spirit as you walk with Jesus. Go back to the point of your very conception.

The Bible is clear in stating that the Lord knew you even before you physically existed. God's concern for you began before you were born. He was there, even in that first moment of conception, caring for you and protecting you. Before you pray this prayer, get your Bible and read Psalm 139:1-17.

Jesus has been with you all the time! He knows you; He loves you. Before you were formed in your mother's womb, Jesus was watching you, loving you, and protecting you.

Take this positive, affirmative thought and hold it tightly in your heart. See Jesus with you in that first moment. See Jesus caressing you and soothing you, even in the womb. If you feel tension or concern over your conception, pray this *healing prayer:*

Dear Jesus, I thank you for being with me, even from the beginning of life. Before I was born, you were with me. You care. Forgive any anger and pain that took place when I was conceived. Forgive any wrong thoughts and wrong actions of my parents. Forgive them for allowing anything negative to destroy the joy of what was a sacred and joyous moment. And Lord, forgive me for any latent resentment I might still hold toward them. Bless them and bless me. Heal this emotional wound.

Visualize Jesus rocking you in His arms and loving you, even before you were born. See Him taking away the sting of all the painful memories of the past.

Note that this is a model prayer—actually bits and pieces of a model prayer. You should feel free to elaborate and modify the specific words to fit your situation. In fact, the more specific you make your prayer, the more effective it will be. Prayer is personal communion between you and the Lord, so be as personal as you can. Name dates and places and events. Name people as they are brought to your mind and then forgive them. Recall the moments as vividly as you can, laying all the details at the Lord's feet and submitting to His healing touch. Make this model prayer your personal prayer for healing.

Heavenly Father, thank you for creating me as a living, breathing personality who is made in your image and by your love. I am thankful that it was your will for me to be born. Lord Jesus, thank you for being there from the very conception of my life.

Lord, with this knowledge and understanding, teach me by your Spirit to become completely alive and whole. Take me back in the Spirit to relive and release those events in the past that could be used by the Enemy to weaken or hinder the expression of your character through my personality.

By the power of your Holy Spirit, set me free from any feelings of unworthiness or sense of being unloved. Thank you for loving me, Jesus. May the beauty of your love replace the ashes of self-condemnation.

Visualizing Your Childhood

Continue moving through your life into your childhood. Be sensitive as the Spirit points out various situations that may have been harmful. At each one, stop and visualize Jesus with you at that moment and pray the healing prayer. Forgive all those involved. Confess your own hostilities and resentments; release any festering anger. Let Jesus bless the moment and heal the pain.

As you continue to visualize yourself walking through your past, pray for each painful moment as it is recalled:

Father, walk me through my childhood, through those early years, and heal the harsh memories I've stored from those times. Heal the pain that's followed me through the years and kept me from full joy in you. Remove the barriers of my past that have robbed me of present blessings. Redeem my mind and memories as you have already redeemed my past and my sins.

Name each incident as the Holy Spirit brings it to your mind: separations from parents because of sickness or death, unloving families, divorces, physical hurts, traumas of various kinds, and so on.

Picture Christ sitting at the head of the family table when you were a child. Picture Him moving from place to place around the table, touching each head and anointing each life with His love.

Jesus was there then. You may not have realized it at the time, but He was there. Now that you are legally and spiritually His child, you have the right and the power to go back into your past. Now you can reprogram your subconscious and reconstruct those personal memories with Jesus included. That's what the Lord will do for you as He continues to walk you through your past.

Redeeming The Past

Before you accepted Christ as your personal Savior, you had committed many sins and made many mistakes. As a result, your present circumstances and personality were shaped by the wrong decisions you made. Jesus forgives your sins and redeems your past, clearing away the present and future for the fullness of His joy.

This "redeeming of your past" means that Jesus considers what *was* as what *should have been*. He doesn't look back at your redeemed past and see your sins and mistakes. Your sinful past no longer exists except in your own memory! That is why it is so important to allow your memory to be redeemed just as your past has been. If this does not occur, even though your sins have been erased, the effects of those sins will still continue through the power of your unhealed memory.

It is imperative to deal with each hurt and each fear, no matter how insignificant you consider it to be. If it is fear, it needs to be erased from your memory. If it is hurt, you need to let the Lord heal the pain:

Lord Jesus, by your Spirit, enter the innermost part of my personality. Allow the warm glow of your presence to reaffirm your peace, love, hope, joy, and protection to my soul. By faith I believe that no weapon formed against me will prosper.

Dispel all the childhood fears remaining in my life. Walk back with me to school, Lord, and show me your presence during those moments when I was embarrassed or treated harshly, when classmates called me names, when I was belittled and picked on. You were there, Jesus, all the time. Bless those moments and take away the sting of hurt.

Heal every scar that keeps me from reaching out today. Heal me of everything that blocks my communication with you and others. Reconstruct my personality. Heal all relationships from the moment they began, even in my childhood. Heal me of the fears that entered my life in the later school years: fear of speaking in public, fear of looking incompetent, fear of not being loved or not being able to love.

Lord, put within my heart a security to know that I can step out for you, that I can speak for you, that I can express your love to others without fear of rejection. They rejected your Son, but He rose above that—and now, with your help, let me rise above it, too. Thank you, Father.

As you ask God to forgive those who have hurt you,

you are erasing the pain recorded on those old sub-conscious tapes. Walking with Jesus back through your past re-records those tapes with Him in the picture. Then, only one step remains: playing back those old tapes. To accomplish that, you need to pray through a prayer similar to the one I have provided.

What's the normal procedure for prayer for personality reconstruction? There really is none. I have never followed precisely the same pattern for any two people with whom I've prayed. It is imperative that the Spirit lead. Many times I've been prompted to pray in a completely different way than I have before. Scripture, experience, and the Holy Spirit give the guidelines that are discussed in this book.

Suppressed memories are painful, and it is helpful when a fellow Christian prays with the person in need. Most people find it better to have someone from outside their normal circle of acquaintances pray with them. This provides greater freedom as well as added objectivity. Some people can't hear the Lord because of their own pain. Having no preconceived notions concerning the person's past and present allows the counselor to be objective, relying completely on the Lord for the word of knowledge and direction.

Points To Remember

1. Jesus is love and light. He can redeem the most unpleasant memories in the same way He forgives your sins of long ago.

2. Begin your inner healing with a prayer of confession and confirmation.
3. Jesus has been with you all the time. He knows you, and He loves you. Before you were formed, Jesus was watching, loving, and protecting you.
4. Thank God for the miracle He is about to perform in your life.
5. Accept the Lord's healing as He touches each moment of your past.
6. Jesus forgives your sins and redeems your past, clearing away the present and future for the fullness of His joy.

Chapter 6

TAKE RESPONSIBILITY FOR CHANGE

The original sin, committed by Adam and Eve, was *rebellion*. Rebellion is at the root of all other sins and all symptoms of sin. Rebellion can manifest itself in believers' lives as well as in the lives of unbelievers. Since God has come to set up His Kingdom in our hearts, we can never have His abundance until we eliminate all rebellion from our hearts.

We can see common threads of sin in every person's life—and all throughout human history. Because of sin, God cursed the life of this world with hardship. (See Genesis 3:17-19.) Man's nature was corrupted, and his conscience was filled with guilt. From that guilty conscience comes emotional illness, psychosomatic disease, anxiety, muscular tension, and so forth.

Adam ran and hid. His corrupt nature drove him to avoid a confrontation with God. Proverbs 28:1 says that the wicked flee when no man pursues! We still do it today. We try to hide the areas of our lives that we know God desires to change.

Many of us try to shift the blame for our sin. Adam tried this ploy in the Garden of Eden: "The woman made me do it."

Eve tried to pass the buck, too: "The serpent made me do it."

We are still doing it today: "My parents raised me this way." Or, "I was vulnerable at the time." Or, "I wasn't responsible; it was my spouse's fault."

God's Word tells us we are responsible for our actions. We can't shift the blame and say, "God, why did you do this to me?" We can't blame God or anyone else. God doesn't *do* anything to us; He allows us to choose our own actions and *do* to ourselves. When we refuse to take responsibility for our own actions, we are raising our fists to God—rebelling against Him and His Word. We are calling God a liar and denying His forgiveness and mercy.

Over the years, I have counseled many people. It is interesting to note that, although every situation is different, the excuses people give are similar.

Counselee Remarks:	Appropriate Counselor Responses:
I can't do it.	Don't say can't. With God all things are possible. Will you try or won't you?
Make me better, I dare you.	You must be willing to be well. I will help by directing you to the answer.

86

It's their fault.	What part did you play in their actions?
Doctor, I had bad parents.	Life is not always perfect; what are you going to make out of your life today?
They don't understand me.	Can't you think of someone who does?
It's not that simple.	God's way may sound simple, but a change in attitude is so important.
I'm too old to change.	God made you in His likeness. He designed you so you could change.
It's my nature.	True, but God commands you to take on a new nature.
It won't work.	It won't, or is it that you don't try?

Discouragement has a way of interrupting your course in life. If you lose hope and think that success is impossible, you will fall into a desperate state of depression.

As Christians, our hope of glory is *change*—change that Jesus brings because He is willing to continue changing us, working with us, molding us, and loving us for who we are.

Jude spoke of this at the end of his epistle: "Now unto him that is able to keep you from falling, and to present you faultless before the presence of his glory with exceeding joy, to the only wise God our Saviour, be glory and majesty, dominion and power, both now and forever. Amen'' (verse 25).

From the beginning of the world, God promised that Christ would come and defeat sin—so there was always hope for change. But change is even more possible today since Christ has defeated evil on the cross.

The Freedom Of Discipline

There are two styles of living: *emotion-oriented* living and *disciple-oriented* living. If you let emotions alone motivate what you do and say, you are living with reversed priorities and are failing to follow Christ's plan for your life. God wants you to be obedient to the commandments He has given in His Word, regardless of whether you feel like it or not. Generally though, when you obey God, feelings will follow.

Many people pray and pray but never step out and act in faith—they never experience what God has promised. They are trapped by the tyranny of their feelings. Living by feelings is living without discipline.

Discipline brings freedom. Most people believe that discipline and freedom are opposites—that they are mutually exclusive. Yet, without discipline, you merely exist instead of truly live. Discipline allows you to tap into the talents and the abilities that lie dormant and wasted within you.

What does discipline mean? To be disciplined in the Christian life means to be the Lord's disciple. Being disciplined means reading the Bible and praying daily. To be disciplined means to accept Christ's healing in your life and to live victoriously—free from the tyranny of feelings.

Faithful discipline will turn you around. It will cause you to bring that area of disobedience in your life to the Lord and prompt you to say, "Lord, take this area and change it according to your will." Discipline creates within you the *desire* to want to change.

The Changemaker

"Jesus can conquer anything, but there's no way I can ever change!"

This is the way many Christians think. They acknowledge God's omnipotence in every realm of life, except within themselves. Satan has debilitated them with an overblown impression of their limitations. They cannot apply the simple but powerful principles of God's divine omnipotence to their personalities!

Essentially, what they are saying (without realizing it) is that God can't be true to His own Word. To deny God's power and authority in one area is to deny God in all things. Paul addresses the subject in 1 Corinthians 10:13: "There hath no temptation taken you but such as is common to man: but God is faithful, who will not suffer you to be tempted above that ye are able; but will with the temptation also make a way to escape, that ye may be able to bear it.''

God always has an angle for conquest—or at least an escape—in every circumstance. He will not allow circumstances to be the excuse for failure in a Christian's life.

People who have been through Alcoholics Anonymous (AA) and similar programs have learned this concept. They went through life saying, ''Aw, I got a bum deal . . . my parents did this and that to me . . . I was a victim in my situation . . . Everything was fine until I met that guy . . .'' and so on. They have the distorted belief that God has given them a worse set of circumstances than other people. Actually, their problems are no different than anyone else's. Instead, circumstances should be taken as teaching tools and turned into assets. This is the constructive way in which to handle all problems.

God wants your heart in tune with Him—not with your circumstances. Once your heart is in tune with Him, you'll be able to deal more effectively with whatever circumstances come your way.

Tribulation, whether self or other-inflicted, brings the real you to the surface. It reveals what is in your heart—the part you've denied exists. This is the one reason persecution is a standard for the Church—to reveal the flaws and the shreds of the ''old man'' nature that linger. Through such trials we discover where we are still vulnerable to attack by the Enemy.

We can then allow the Holy Spirit to make changes, to strengthen us, to fortify those vulnerable areas of our personalities.

Some Christians struggle with habits that change slowly. Why? Because there is so much of the old man to be disposed of! The Spirit of God must be allowed to restructure your life, your thinking, and your whole personality. This is usually a gradual process and not an instant, miraculous change.

God insists on your partnership in the effort. He requires the discipline of the learning process. You must choose to replace old habits and old thinking with new, godly traits. You must replace the old pattern of behavior with a new one. All this comes with discipline, training, and hard work.

Nobody will force you to change. Nobody will make you choose to change. The choice has to come from your own heart.

When the alcoholic attends an AA meeting, he is made to realize that there are a lot of people who have suffered as much or more than he has. In many cases, this awareness is the key to his turnaround. He sees that others have experienced grief just as he has, and yet here they are, sitting in the same room—not beyond hope.

Likewise, as Christians, we know that no person is past the point of God's redemption. God always wants what is best for you. When God sees a spark of willingness in your heart, He takes action immediately.

Toys In The Attic

Some Christians spend years playing games with God. "Should I stop doing this or that?" they pray insincerely. They feel the Holy Spirit convicting them, but they won't give up that one weak area. I call these weak areas "toys in the attic" because we love to play with them. But this is a dangerous game. The day may come when that playful area infects your life like a cancer.

The "toy" may not be bad in itself, but because it takes precedence over your love for God, it must be eliminated. As long as you cling to this toy, it will limit the work of the Spirit in your life.

James wrote about the person who keeps "toys in the attic." He said, "A double minded man is unstable in all his ways" (James 1:8).

Double-mindedness destroys the efforts of Christians to serve God. It has ruined many prominent Christian men and women with outstanding public ministries. Why? Because there was that one little area, that one toy in the attic that they failed to surrender wholly to Christ.

I had a young friend, an unbeliever, who rebelled against the traditional values of his godly parents to become a rock-and-roll star. He was on the way to achieving his goal when he found Christ as his Savior. God told him to abandon his career in music. This young man's talent was a good thing in and of itself, and his success was undeniable. But that seed of rebellion had been allowed to flourish through the years, and God needed to replace it with single-minded obedience. The infection had to be cut out so that God could heal that inflamed area of this young man's personality.

Look back over your own life. What has God asked you to relinquish? Perhaps you were a little stubborn about it at first, or maybe you tried to rationalize your rebellion. If you obeyed, you know the blessings that have come from that obedience. If you failed to obey, you know the heartache that has resulted.

Double-mindedness is the mud and muck of life. Single-mindedness is solidly resting on God's Word and God's will. It is the rock of life. The foundation of your personality must be built upon God's Word and God's will.

Memory Joggers

The foundation of your personality is the accumulation of lessons you've had to learn the hard way. Can you remember a time you procrastinated and the result that followed? Can you remember the last time you quit a task out of frustration, failing to lean on the Lord? What was the result? All sorts of these memories reside in your mind, and they are an important part of the foundation of your personality. They remind you to achieve more highly in the present and the future. That's why God gave you a memory.

Many times, in an effort to expand my practice,

I have stepped out in faith financially. When bills needed to be paid, I often had to play the game of "bob and weave." I would *bob* accounts and *weave* a pattern in order to make the necessary payments. With God's help, I would arrive at a satisfactory solution just minutes before the final deadline. This is not always a pleasant way to live, but it is exciting to see God answer prayer and come through at the last moment.

Today, when times of testing come, I can look back on past experiences and remind myself of God's faithfulness.

The Lord often tests your faith and trustworthiness by placing obstacles in your path from time to time. When you remember how you have successfully dealt with such circumstances in the past—on the strength of God's Word—you become willing to step out in faith, demonstrating your trust in God and thanking Him for every trial as a gift!

Present-Time Conscious

Many people squander their mental, emotional, physical, and spiritual resources on anxiety over the past or future. But God's attitude focuses on the present. The past is unchangeable; the future is not promised to anybody. Today is a gift from God. It is yours to use. Make it count for Christ. Concentrate on the present not on the past or the future.

Anxiety, worry, and doubts are manifestations of

one thing: *fear*. Fear is a hiding, self-protection impulse that goes back to the Garden of Eden when Adam and Eve fled from the presence of God.

Fear fails to take responsibility today. But *love*, conversely, looks for opportunity to give. It asks, "What can I do for someone else?" It labors long and is busy all the time. A loving attitude has no time to worry about tomorrow.

Love is the opposite of fear. "Herein is our love made perfect, that we may have boldness in the day of judgment: because as he is, so are we in this world. There is no fear in love, but perfect love casteth out fear: because fear hath torment. He that feareth is not made perfect in love" (1 John 4:17-18).

It's a mathematical formula: *As love increases, boldness increases, and fear decreases.* When fear abounds in the heart, then the Biblical principle of love is not perfect. It's not complete.

But "as he is, so are we in this world," John writes. The Holy Spirit will give us boldness in the present to do God's will here on earth.

The psalmist talked about fear in Psalm 112: "Praise ye the Lord. Blessed is the man that feareth the Lord, that delighteth greatly in his commandments . . . .He shall not be afraid of evil tidings: his heart is fixed, trusting in the Lord. His heart is established, he shall not be afraid, until he see his desire upon his enemies" (112:1,7-8).

Jesus defeated the Enemy in the wilderness with the Word of God. God's promises will not fail. As you apply God's Word to your heart, as you make His Word live in your life, God's power will be present in your situation.

We are told to put on "the whole armor of God" and to take "the sword of the Spirit, which is the word of God" (Ephesians 6:11,17). By confessing God's Word positively in faith, we can stand our ground against the Enemy and live victoriously in every area of our lives. Make this never-again list a memorized part of your armor.

My "Never Again" List (by Don Gossett)

1. Never again will I confess "I can't," for "I can do all things through Christ which strengtheneth me" (Philippians 4:13).
2. Never again will I confess lack, for "my God shall supply all my need according to his riches in glory by Christ Jesus" (Philippians 4:19).
3. Never again will I confess fear, for "God hath not given me the spirit of fear, but of power, and of love, and of a sound mind" (2 Timothy 1:7).
4. Never again will I confess doubt and lack of faith, for "God hath given to every man the measure of faith" (Romans 12:3).
5. Never again will I confess weakness, for "the Lord is the strength of my life" (Psalm 27:1). "The people that know their God shall be strong and do exploits" (Daniel 11:32).
6. Never again will I confess supremacy of Satan

over my life, for "greater is he that is within me than he that is in the world" (1 John 4:4).

7. Never again will I confess defeat, for "God always causeth me to triumph in Christ" (2 Corinthians 2:14).

8. Never again will I confess lack of wisdom, for "Christ Jesus is made unto me wisdom from God" (1 Corinthians 1:30).

9. Never again will I confess sickness, for "with his stripes I am healed" (Isaiah 53:5). Jesus "Himself took my infirmities, and bare my sickness" (Matthew 8:17).

10. Never again will I confess worries and frustrations, for I am "casting all my cares upon him; for he careth for me" (1 Peter 5:7). In Christ I am "care-free."

11. Never again will I confess bondage, for "where the Spirit of the Lord is, there is liberty" (2 Corinthians 3:17). My body is the temple of the Holy Spirit.

12. Never again will I confess condemnation, for "there is therefore now no condemnation to them which are in Christ Jesus" (Romans 8:1). I am in Christ; therefore, I am free from condemnation.

Points To Remember

1. Rebellion is at the root of all other sins and all symptoms of sin.

2. Since God has come to set up His Kingdom in your heart, you can never have His abundance until you eliminate all rebellion from your heart.

3. Living by feelings is living without discipline. Serve God out of a heart of obedience.

4. Discipline brings freedom. Without discipline, you merely exist instead of truly live.

5. Choose to replace old habits and old thinking with new, godly traits. Replace the old pattern of behavior with a new one.

6. Double-mindedness destroys the efforts of Christians to serve God. Single-mindedness is solidly resting on God's Word and God's will.

7. God's attitude focuses on the present. The past is unchangeable; the future is not promised to anybody. Today is a gift from God.

8. As love increases, boldness increases, and fear decreases.

Chapter 7

CHANGING YOUR HABIT PATTERNS

You can break bad habits! But you must be willing to take control of your life and not allow old habits to control you. The way to begin the process of change is to take inventory of your lifestyle.

Diagnose your own self-defeating behavior, then treat the "old man." Look at your habits. Look at the patterns you have established. Most of them probably seem quite normal—just a regular part of your personality.

The old man within us doesn't like to have his heart inspected. He does not feel comfortable with introspection. He does not like the hard work of living by God's Word. Obedience doesn't come easy to the old nature.

God can change your desires as you allow Him to, but change must begin in the heart. You can be anointed with gallons of oil, but without a willing heart, healing will evade you. Desire, discipline, and true repentance are absolutely necessary.

Discover God's remedy, then prescribe it to your

self-defeating behavior. Go to God's Word and find out what He has to say about the areas of weakness in your life. Then, ask the Holy Spirit to help you change those areas.

Sometimes we must learn the same lesson again and again until we get it right. This is how God deals with us, patiently, lovingly, but persistently. It's a continuous, gradual process.

When is a thief not a thief? When he's not stealing? Some would say so. But when is a drug addict not a drug addict? When he's not presently taking drugs?

A drug addict is no longer a drug addict when he has become something else. And a thief is no longer a thief when something in him has changed. The sinner must not only stop sinning, but he must put on new habit patterns and change his behavior. Then he must maintain the change in his life. The new way of living must be actively pursued. You must discipline yourself to the new lifestyle, the new thought process, and the new response pattern.

Place quality control in your life. Don't allow one area of your life to drag you down in other areas. If you have trouble taking time for Bible study, for example, don't study near the TV set, where you'll be tempted to turn God off and turn the set on. Study far away from any distractions.

Concentrate on your prayer life. No greater single tool exists for change in your life than communication with your heavenly Father. Prayer will blend the Father's heart with yours. If you don't have a prayer life, you won't have much of a Christian life.

Pray positively. Negative prayers can do more harm than good. Avoid self-pity. Surrender every problem and every unhappiness to Him. Pray thankfully. In your prayer time, set aside a portion for praise only.

Eradicate sin by spiritual surgery. When a negative thought enters your mind, dismiss it immediately. Don't ponder it or toy with it, mulling it over again and again. That's how the fruit of the tree finally got the better of Eve. The thought became a desire because Eve let it slip from her mind down into her heart.

Take inventory daily. See what's in your heart. Get alone with God and get rid of everything that has no business there. The thought that becomes a desire becomes an act, and the act that becomes a habit becomes slavery.

Don't be afraid to cry for help. The modern Christian has trouble with this. We put on a facade of self-sufficiency, but God's Word tells us to confess our faults and our needs to one another.

When I played football, the guys would seldom confess they were hurt on a play unless it was obvious. A player would have to be knocked unconscious before he'd admit his weakness. Males, more often than females, have been taught that admitting pain or weakness is demasculizing. We limp along through life never properly dealing with areas that need special attention.

You may not feel comfortable crying out for help, but it could be the first step toward reconstruction of your life. Be willing to admit you have an identifiable problem worthy of attention and that you don't have all the answers. If you maintain a teachable spirit, you'll be able to receive valuable help and advice from other people.

Ask someone who's victorious in a certain area to help you achieve victory in that area, too. If you feel you need further counseling, make an appointment to see your pastor or a Christian psychologist.

Practice your new behavior. Exercise your spirit. Repeat the new habit patterns until they become such a part of you that it's natural.

Be patient. Change takes time. With some people, three weeks of active work will result in good progress. For others, the breaking-in period will be longer, or it could be shorter. But don't give up after one or two days, or a week.

Keep working at it. Your discipline now will give you freedom later on. Someday soon, you'll discover that your every thought has been brought into captivity to the obedience of Christ.

Eliminating Negative Attitudes

Did you know that most illnesses—emotionally, spiritually, and physically—can be healed by a proper attitude toward life?

Life is a series of choices. Most reactions to our environment create different responses in different individuals. In every life crisis, you can choose the end result of that situation. By your will, you establish the final outcome to be one of two consequences: victory or depression.

Victory is achieved by active forgiveness and ongoing lovingkindness. Choosing to forgive others, with God's help, sets your emotions free to pursue positive goals and activities. When you walk in love and kindness toward people, victory becomes a natural part of your lifestyle.

Depression can result when you experience an emotional injury, insult, or rejection. If a negative experience becomes combined with anger, revenge, resentment, and self-pity, depression is sure to follow.

What event or experience in your life cripples you the most? Start to see that event from God's viewpoint. Work with it until you can see that negative situation as a positive gift.

Nothing—no situation—is without hope.

All negative emotions and self-images can be healed and changed through the proper application of God's Word plus time and discipline. (See Philippians 3:14; John 8:31-32).

To attract the abundant life you must eliminate:

Fear of the future.

Worry over the past.

Anxiety for the present.

These emotions are a waste of time. To eliminate fear, worry, and anxiety, you must bring "into captivity every thought to the obedience of Christ" (2 Corinthians 10:5).

Learn to abandon these *negative attitudes:*
Worry over being misunderstood.
Clinging to false assumptions.
Being unnecessarily serious.
Regretting the past.
Disliking yourself.
Hating the process and stages of life.

How A Thought Becomes A Habit

A thought (either positive or negative) can be re-buked or accepted. When a thought is accepted, it becomes emotionalized as a strong desire in your heart. At this stage you are compelled to act. If this act is continued, it becomes a habit and a part of your personality.

How a thought becomes part of your personality:

THOUGHT	*Origin*—choosing stage. You can choose to rebuke or accept the thought.
DESIRE	If accepted, the thought becomes *emotionalized*.
ACT	Once emotionalized, an idea must be *acted* upon.
HABIT	Action becomes *routine*.
PERSONALITY	Habit forms an *attitude*.
DESTINY	Determines where you will spend *eternity*.

The Bible warns us that those who feed their minds with evil ideas eventually are overcome with these desires to the point where they act them out. Bad habits become routine and lead to the formation of a reprobate character. The Bible declares in Romans 1:28 that at this point it takes a mighty miracle of God's deliverance to free this person. A reprobate has lost his shame of sin and encourages others to do the same.

Negative emotions can become bad habits and these should be avoided. *Jealousy, revenge, greed,* and *superstition,* if left uncontrolled, can lead to *fear, anger,* and *hatred.*

Never let your inner personality be dominated by these negative emotions. Let your heart and mind be filled with constructive thoughts and attitudes.

Bind Satan in Jesus' name, then paralyze him with God's Word. Order him out of the affairs of your life. All negative emotions can be healed and changed in time through the proper application of God's Word and with discipline. (See Philippians 3:14; John 8:31-32.)

The Word of God will help wash away the bad mental-emotional habits and bring your spirit in line with the Word of God. Jesus said, "Now ye are clean through the word I have spoken unto you" (John 15:3). He is able to sanctify and cleanse us by "the washing of the word" (Ephesians 5:26).

Transforming Your Thought Patterns

God will transform your personality as you are faithful to put His Word into action. Begin today to believe and achieve God's plan and purpose for your life. Negative thought patterns, attitudes, and habits can be changed by following these steps:

1. Decide which habits or attitudes you want to change.
2. Write the goals you want to attain in each area.
3. Share your goals with someone in prayer. Two or more agreeing together has a powerful effect. (Read Matthew 18:19.) But be careful to pray with someone positive and supportive of your life's goals.
4. Lock into the vision by exercising Mark 11:23-24. Believe these verses as realities in your heart, then confess them daily out loud.

Positive emotional confessions unlock the negative subconscious part of your personality. The *major positive emotions* of *faith, hope,* and *love,* if allowed to develop properly, will create *constructive desire, proper sexual expression, enthusiasm,* and *romance.* Master these emotions, and you will be able to control your other feelings.

Our minds and emotions must be involved whenever we pray. *Prayer* brings about change in our lives and personalities. Use the following steps to obtain a positive answer to your prayers:

Confirm from God's Word that what you want is His desire for you and that it is attainable.

Visualize the answer in your mind's eye, live it, breathe it, and exercise it many times. Stay relaxed, calm, and assured.

Confess the answer by speaking positively about what you believe God is going to do for you. See God delivering your prayer to you.

Keep faith at the door of your mind. Don't waver and never doubt.

Receive God's answer in Jesus' name.

When you pray, avoid struggle and strain, since this attitude indicates unbelief or fear that what you desire is not God's will. It is the quiet spirit that gets things done. Unclutter your mind. Tell it to be still, and it will obey you.

Learn to let go and relax. You can float on water if you remain quiet, still, and at peace. But if you get nervous or fearful, you will sink. In your prayer time, be at peace with yourself and God. Start first with praise and worship to quiet your spirit. Then identify yourself with the Giver of life and love, and feel yourself swimming in the great ocean of God's love. The Lord will restore your soul and reconstruct your personality through prayer.

Pray the following prayer on a daily basis, and you will begin to see positive and miraculous changes take place in your personality and your life.

Today is your day, Lord, and with your help it will be a glorious day for me—full of love, joy, peace, longsuffering, gentleness, goodness, and truth. My truth is in your goodness, Father. The right outcome of my actions is written in my heart and emotionalized in my inner personality. I am absolutely convinced that you hear my prayers. According to your perfect law, I believe you attract into my life all the good things my heart desires.

I am at peace when I hear you call into the innermost part of my personality, "Come unto me, all ye that labour and are heavy laden, and I will give you rest." I now rest in you, Lord, and know that all is well. The petty things of life no longer irritate me. When fear, worry, and doubt knock at my door, faith in goodness, truth, and beauty will open the door; and there is no one there. O God, thou art my God, and there is none else. Amen.

God's Training Ground

Learn to thank the Lord for allowing you to cope and deal with every problem in your life. The Lord is working for your good. He sees what's ahead, and He is working in you now to prepare you for the future. He is preparing you to be ready for that person or that circumstance or that revelation that will make great demands on you later.

Getting through each day by thanking God for your ability to cope with problems is a way of proving God's Word in the little things of life. Then, when the great challenges come, you'll be fully conditioned—like a boxer who has trained for months for a big match.

Don't give up. Your faith, if it is true faith, is strong enough to keep you plodding through times of trial and testing! Those experiences, no matter how unpleasant, will secure you and anchor you.

Faith grows through time. You don't become the president of a great corporation by walking through the front door in a pin-striped suit saying, "Here I am!" You begin on the assembly line, on the loading dock, on the ground floor, learning each day and growing in understanding, skill, and vision. The same is true with faith. You learn from your experiences over time, and your faith grows.

God is building a people who will have the strength to be separate and holy, even in times of adversity.

Life will keep throwing you curves until you learn how to respond to them. You'll encounter the same problems repeatedly until you conquer them in Christ. This is God's way of training you. You don't graduate to high school until you've mastered grade school and junior high. You don't get the big opportunities for ministry or the big challenges of faith until the little daily challenges have been handled well and your faith has been tried and found true.

Points To Remember

1. God can change your desires as you allow Him to, but change must begin in your heart.
2. Concentrate on your prayer life. There is no greater single tool for change than communication with your heavenly Father.
3. The thought that becomes a desire becomes an act, and the act that becomes a habit becomes slavery.
4. Life is a series of choices. In every life crisis, you can choose the end result of victory or depression.
5. To eliminate fear, worry, and anxiety, you must bring every thought into captivity to the obedience of Christ.
6. God will transform your personality as you are faithful to put His Word into action.

Chapter 8

A HEALTHY SELF-IMAGE

Self-acceptance is at the heart of a healthy self-image. Everyone needs to be accepted—it's an in-bred characteristic—but the Christian must find his acceptance in Christ.

The self-concept of the believer focuses not on what he is in himself but on what he is in Christ. You are not great or worthy because of the things you do or because you have a wonderful personality. You're great and worthy because of what Christ is doing through you. It is a spiritual inheritance based on your salvation and not an accomplishment based on your efforts.

Self-acceptance is knowing who you are in Christ. When you see yourself created in God's image, lovingly obeying God's commandments, you'll begin to accept yourself because God has made you. You are regenerated by the Spirit of God; you are a member of the family of God; you are forgiven of all iniquity. You are identified with Jesus Christ, and you are destined for an eternal inheritance in the presence of God. That's identity enough for anyone! As a Christian, you know who you are.

Failing to accept and value yourself grieves the Spirit of God. Failing to value yourself leads to devaluing others around you. When your normal, daily shortcomings are blown out of proportion, you tend to do the same with the faults of others. This is the result of a poor self-image and lack of self-acceptance. But when the Holy Spirit infiltrates your life, you'll be able to put your failings in proper perspective, lay them on the altar, and move ahead in the joy of God's forgiveness and love.

A healthy self-image must come from the inside out. Many people hold negative images of themselves in their minds. Those images need to be erased and replaced.

Dispelling Inferiority

Do you know who you are in Christ and how God can use you? Or are you still full of self-limiting, debilitating self-concepts? Do you feel that God can't use you in His Kingdom?

Learn to come against your own inhibitions and complexes. You learned them once, and you learned them on your own. Now you must and *can* unlearn them. You have the power to do so because you now have Jesus living inside you!

Your self-image didn't really come from you. For the most part, it is a reflection based on the responses of others toward you. People bombarded you, from the moment of your birth, with opinions about yourself. As you sorted through those impressions, you kept some and discarded others. Without filtering every impression through the Holy Spirit, you latched onto the negative impressions and threw the positive ones away. You learned what you believed were your handicaps and limitations, but you forgot your God-given strengths and talents.

This process affects your relationships with the body of believers. You may try to emulate the most charismatic personality in the church or the most attractive or the most popular. When you don't measure up to that individual's characteristics, you consider yourself a useless failure in God's Kingdom.

You may think you're not good-looking enough to speak publicly or not educated enough to teach a class. You may have decided you can never be anybody because of your background. Yet God is answering each of these objections with His Word, and nothing is impossible with Him.

You have great usefulness in the Kingdom awaiting you—but you must claim your new, healed personality from God. You can claim a new self-image from God because He has promised to give it to you. But He will not force anything on you.

It's like having a package waiting for you at the post office. In order to receive it, you must go pick it up. You have an inheritance from your heavenly Father, but you must claim it. It's yours—tagged with your name—but you must accept it.

Your sense of inferiority is a false one. It flies in

the face of God's omnipotence and grace. "I can do all things through Christ," the apostle Paul declared emphatically. Your preconceived limitations are imaginary; they are not of God. God doesn't see them. When He looks at you, He sees Jesus in you. God did not create a race of failures.

Discipline your mind by training it to see yourself as Jesus sees you, to think as Jesus thinks, to respond the way Jesus responds. You will find your limitations—real or imagined—melting away and being miraculously healed. And you will be on your way to a healthy self-image.

As you abide in Christ and He abides in you, your life will begin to produce good fruit. It will begin bearing fruit in the areas you thought were fruitless. Why? Because you are proving God's Word. You are claiming your inheritance by simple obedience and childlike belief.

Through Christ you are accepted and approved. Let your prayer be:

Father, help me to see myself as you see me. Forgive me for thinking so little of myself. Help me to improve my self-image as I find greater acceptance in your Son, Jesus Christ. I give back to you the gifts and talents you have put within me. Use them in your Kingdom and for your glory. Amen.

Healing For Your Self-Image

A healthy self-image does not happen automatically. You need to take some active steps toward receiving healing of any negative impressions you have of yourself. The most important step involves proper discipline of your mind. Train your mind to see yourself as Jesus sees you, to think as Jesus thinks, and to respond the way Jesus responds. Then you will find your limitations—real or imagined— being miraculously healed. Soon you will be on your way to a healthy self-image.

The following exercises will begin the healing process of new self-acceptance and the loving acceptance of others.

1. Use your imagination and your memory to go back into your past. Walk back through your entire life, hand in hand with Jesus. As each unpleasant experience is brought to your mind, see Jesus there nurturing and loving you. See Him there each time you gained a negative impression of yourself. He was there, and He saw you much differently in that moment than you saw yourself. Visualize the difference His being there makes. Approach the times of failure in your life, and see yourself successful in those situations because Jesus is there with you. Picture each scene as vividly as possible. This will make the spiritual, emotional, and mental impressions stronger and more real. You are creating new material for your mental tape recorder that will replace the negative images. As you find your acceptance in Jesus, your life will begin to produce fruit in those areas you thought were fruitless.

2. Take a pad of paper and a pencil, and spend

some time writing down your strengths, gifts, and talents. Identify what is already good about yourself. Ask God to help you see the good things, and He will bring them to your mind.

3. If you have children, take time every night before they go to sleep to reinforce the idea that you love them. Thank them for something good they did during the day. Stroke your love into them, and it will shape their lives in a beautiful way. Just by letting them know they are accepted and loved, you will be programming their hearts to resist some of the negative input they are bound to get as they go along in life.

4. Pray with your spouse. This can be the most effective means of healing in your life. Pray for your partner's healing and growth, and your own healing will begin. If you are not married, pray with a close friend. You need someone to share with intimately on a spiritual level.

The Proper Mental Attitude

How would you describe a healthy, whole person? The qualities that best describe a healthy person go beyond outward physical signs. Healthy people display the following characteristics in their personalities.

1. *Healthy people display an honest evaluation of themselves.* They have matured to the place where they can evaluate their strengths and define their weak areas. Emotionally well people have learned

to be transparent and can even laugh at some of their imperfections.

2. *Healthy people are not trapped in a twilight zone.* They have a good perspective of what is real and what is not. They maintain the balance between fantasy and reality. Healthy people can dream yet still be practical. They are rational, sane, creative, optimistic, and fanciful, yet they do not suffer hallucinations or delusions of grandeur.

3. *Healthy people have forgiven themselves.* They have sensibly analyzed their attitudes and activities and have come to peace with who they are. Healthy people are not consumed by an internal civil war that robs them of their ability to be presently productive. Forgiven people are not overcome by false guilt, regrets, or rejections that could shut down their internal power supply. These individuals realize that the person of the past is not the person of the present because they have experienced forgiveness through Jesus Christ.

4. *Healthy people display enthusiasm for at least one area of life.* They get excited and show signs of energy and interest in personal projects. People who are creatively involved in doing good or caring for someone special generate a healthy personality. Their lives display commitment to an idea, a philosophy, a theology, or a person.

5. *Healthy people have learned to feel comfortable with loving relationships.* They do not feel threatened by close encounters of the loving kind. Their hearts have remained soft although they could

117

have allowed them to be hardened by hurt and disappointment. Healthy people are not embarrassed to admit their need to love and to be loved. Compliments flow freely from their hearts because they have learned the secret of openly praising others. Loving others is part of their lifestyle—they do not love simply by choice or selection.

6. *Healthy people take charge of their life.* People who are emotionally whole do not continue to blame others for their lack of personal achievement. They do not envy others because they realize their own potential for being successful. These individuals have silenced their alibis and accept personal responsibility for any setbacks. People who are persistent, balanced, and in control have learned this simple secret, "As a man thinketh in his heart, so is he" (Proverbs 23:7).

7. *Healthy people don't assume guilt or take responsibility for events beyond their control.* They try to change the things they can and accept the things they cannot change. They do not carry the weight of the world on their shoulders. Well-adjusted individuals have learned to "cast all their cares" on God because they know He cares about them. When trouble comes, they seek positive solutions to their problems, trusting the Lord for wisdom and strength.

8. *Healthy people do not feel guilty when they relax.* People who have learned balance make sure their work-rest-relaxation time cycle is in proper perspective. Healthy people realize that God loves

them and that He expects them to take time to relax and enjoy life. They see their leisure time as an opportunity to commune with the Lord, enjoy personal interests, and express themselves in creative ways.

9. *Healthy people will not be pressured into giving up their dreams.* They press on to the mark God has set before them. It does not matter what other people think, they are commissioned by the Lord and are determined to do His will. Their goals and objectives in life are not dependent on the approval of family and friends.

10. *Healthy people have an adventurous spirit.* People who are young at heart can remain flexible, loving, and whole. They can take chances and occasional risks. Well-adjusted individuals are interested in fresh ideas, like to discover exciting places, and enjoy meeting new people.

11. *Healthy people can adapt to change.* Healthy people realize that change is inevitable. When change comes, they accept it and don't become overly upset. Well-adjusted individuals are not afraid to form new relationships. They don't isolate themselves behind a wall of yesterdays' successes, but they push on to new horizons. Healthy people pass through life's stages without stagnating at one level. They've fallen in love with the process of life—good times and bad times. Whatever comes their attitude is, ''All things work together for good'' (Romans 8:28).

12. *Healthy people realize their humanness and*

have come to terms with death. They do not run life's course with their head in the sand, avoiding confrontation with this final chapter. Healthy people view death with a certain resolve and peace and are able to get on with living. They know their eternal destiny is secure in the salvation provided through Jesus Christ.

Victorious Living

The reconstruction of your personality is not an end but a beginning. Positive reconstruction brings power into your life, but it is power that must be applied and reapplied. Satan does not give up on you once you come to Christ. He works harder. In your own flesh—by your own power—you can't stand against his incessant battering.

You cannot simply wake up in the morning and decide, "I'm going to be a good guy today," and then succeed merely by the power of your own natural will. Many people think that this is all it takes. But you must lean on Jesus. You must continually work to reprogram your mind with His Word, refusing to give ground to wrong, defeated thinking.

In Galatians 2:20, the apostle Paul writes: "I am crucified with Christ: nevertheless I live; yet not I, but Christ liveth in me: and the life which I now live in the flesh I live by the faith of the Son of God, who loved me, and gave himself for me."

Dying to self and allowing Christ to live in you is the power of the Christian life. Your will comes into play in that you willfully turn yourself over to Christ's Lordship. If you do not continue to surrender yourself to God on a daily basis, your "self" will begin dealing with your problems in a natural, fleshy way. Then you'll return to the old, painful, and defeated lifestyle.

Reconstructing your personality isn't just the application of a few prayer principles. It is the application of disciplined, Biblical, faith-releasing prayer and practice. Sometimes a person will spend hours in prayer, but his praying centers on "self" and his "miserable" condition. He wallows in self-pity, and his prayers offend God! "Oh God," he prays, "why did you do this to me?"

It grieves the heart of God when His children fail to claim their inheritance and fail to live in the richness of His full blessing.

The *proper mental attitude* for the victorious Christian must include certain elements:

1. *Be M.A.D. (Motivated and Aggresively Desirous) about living a victorious Christian life.* There has to be a "want-to" if you are to have any good thing from the Lord. God doesn't force a gift on anybody, but He freely gives to all who desire to receive.

2. *Keep your accounts short.* Jimmy Swaggart once compared confession to foot-washing. It's something you have to do each day, but it doesn't mean the whole body is dirty. Confessing your sins daily does not mean you are not saved. It simply means an area of your life isn't in complete line with God's will.

Confession must be a daily exercise. Sin is like cancer. If left untreated, it will grow, take control of your life, and ultimately destroy you. Confess your sins and daily seek God's forgiveness. He never tires of forgiving His children.

3. *Don't wallow in self-pity.* Whether your self-pity is based on reality or fantasy, it must be treated as sin. Whether you deserve the sympathy is not the point. The fact is that focusing on yourself is unhealthy.

Self-pity is as binding as alcoholism or any other drug addiction. It is one of the worst emotional, psychological, and physically-debilitating disorders a person can suffer. Self-pity denies the veracity of Philippians 4:13: "I can do all things through Christ which strengtheneth me."

Your potential for effectiveness in the Kingdom is destroyed because self-pity disregards the very foundation of your faith. It denies the belief that God is in control. Without that basis of faith, you can't even take the first step forward in obedience to God. And without obedience, you are in sin.

Face self-pity for the sin it really is. If you are praying prayers of self-pity, save your breath. God asks us to pray in the power of the Holy Spirit. Out of the abundance of the heart, the mouth speaks. Prayers of self-pity only expose a heart of selfishness.

4. *Develop the positive praise personality.* You should Positively Respond Always In Spiritual Energy (P-R-A-I-S-E).

The life of Job is an example of a man who praised

God in every situation. He praised God even when it looked like God would allow him to be destroyed. (See Job 1:21-22.)

The three Hebrew boys taken to Babylon also had a firm hold on this element of victorious living. They praised God in the fiery furnace—something you and I have never yet experienced. (See Daniel 3:15-25.) Praising in the midst of our comparatively petty problems should be easier for us.

Praise lifts the load. It erases self-pity. It gives you the "want-to." It changes self-centered prayer into healthy, effective, worshipping prayer. God-centered and God-directed prayer is the most powerful tool in the universe.

5. *Develop the discipline of loving forgiveness as a daily exercise.* You have no choice when it comes to forgiveness. Whether or not you forgive is not determined by whether or not someone deserves your forgiveness. Neither is it dependent upon your fears. It is your duty to forgive whether you want to or not!

Christ made this clear in Luke 17:3. He told His disciples that when a brother sinned against them, they were to forgive him. And if he repeated the same offense seven times in a single day, they were to forgive each time and more. In the natural this doesn't make sense. By the third or fourth offense, we would be convinced that real repentance was not happening in this brother's life.

But forgiveness is not dependent upon whether you see the evidence of repentance or not. Forgiveness isn't designed to help the other guy, the offender—it's designed to help you, the offended. Why? Because God wants your heart free from grudges, hate, and old wounds.

Within your heart—your communication link with the Father—is the potential to have the fullness of God. God wants to guarantee that your potential isn't diminished for any reason. Failing to forgive will weaken the link. Forgiveness keeps the channel open.

6. *Conceive and believe in the best possible outcome for all things.* Live expectantly in anticipation of the victory that is imminent. Many people know God answers prayer, but they get frustrated or impatient before the answer is revealed. God doesn't always work instantaneously, even with healing. Yet, He wants you to keep praying and fellowshipping with Him while He works in His own time. The practice of patience as you wait is part of the healing process that leads to maturity and spiritual stability.

If you feel like God isn't going to answer, get a friend to pray with you for thirty minutes once a week. You'll start to see changes—first in your own heart, then in the situation you're praying about.

7. *Learn to guard your mind.* Learn to dispell negative and wrong thoughts rather than dwell on them. To hold onto them will create a craving in your heart for the wickedness you imagine. Once you emotionalize a thought in that way it can easily become a "need"—a drive. Rebuke such thoughts in the name of Jesus.

Speaking positively and cheerfully will help regulate your feelings. You cannot entirely regulate your feelings, but you can influence them by the way you talk. And talking is an indication of how you think. You can talk yourself out of negative responses and into positive actions and forgiveness. This is why praising all the time is so important.

Surrendering To Change

"Jane would look okay if she'd just change the way she dresses. She looks so drab."

"My marriage would be fantastic if only Harry would pay more attention to me."

We spend too much of our energy trying to change other people. What we're actually doing is trying to mold them into our own image and standards. We vainly imagine ourselves to be better than others.

But God instructs us differently! He tells us to change ourselves instead of others.

How many wives have lost their husbands because they demanded that he go to church with her—or else! They were trying to change circumstances *outside* themselves and beyond their control, instead of working on the weaknesses and shortcomings *inside* themselves.

We get caught up in things that will not count for eternity. Many Christians, while they are certainly saved, fail to live in the fullness and the abundance of what God has for them.

God has a plan for your life. You've probably heard that dozens of times. But His plan for you isn't something vague and general. Instead, His plan for you includes specifics.

The key to this abundant life is the surrender of your will—the death of vain goals. Surrender everything, becoming obedient to Christ, regardless of the cost. This is true commitment. Romans 6:11 speaks of dying to self and being alive to Christ. This is the way to be in harmony with God's plan for your life. He will shower you with blessings and spiritual riches.

Points To Remember

1. Self-acceptance is knowing who you are in Christ.
2. You have the power to unlearn your inhibitions and complexes because you have Jesus living inside you.
3. You can claim a new self-image from God because He has promised to give it to you.
4. A healthy self-image must come from the inside out.
5. Dying to self and allowing Christ to live in you is the power of the Christian life. Surrender yourself to God on a daily basis, then your ''self'' won't deal with your problems in a natural, fleshy way.
6. Speaking positively and cheerfully will help regulate your feelings. You can talk yourself out of negative responses and into positive actions and forgiveness.

Chapter 9

GOAL-SETTING AND SUCCESSFUL LIVING

Success is perhaps the most elusive subject in the world. It has been defined and redefined, analyzed and applauded. And still it leaves the world scratching its head.

Christians struggle with the concept of success, too. Perhaps the most common stereotype of a successful Christian life would be someone like evangelist Billy Graham. Many Christians feel they can't accomplish much in the Kingdom because they don't have the notoriety or the clout of an internationally known figure like Graham. They use this feeling as a lame excuse for doing little or nothing. Their lives, by comparison, seem useless and insignificant. They believe that preachers are an elite group free from criticism and problems.

Do not evaluate your success by what other people say or think, or how they react to you. Your success is not measured against what the next guy is accomplishing. Measure success by your willingness to obey what God is calling you to do.

Success, according to God's Word, is more than just an absence of problems. Your most successful times can also be the ones most plagued by persecution, trials, and problems in the natural realm.

One key to success is to thank the Lord regardless of the circumstances. No matter what your mission or your calling, you are going to run into problems that seem to stand in the way of your goal. But in everything give thanks. This practice will build your success rate.

Christ's entire earthly ministry was plagued with criticism. The Pharisees dogged Him throughout His career. His disciples, in whom Jesus invested much time and energy, were still spiritually dull as His earthly ministry came to a close.

People identify success with the things a successful life yields. We strive to buy or attain things we feel will make us happy or keep us healthy. Our goal is the end result of a successful life, so we aim for it, forgetting the path that leads us there. Along the way, we miss the path and fall into a bottomless abyss of materialism, covetousness, and self-deception. By pretending we're happy and successful, the substance behind true happiness and success eludes us.

Success for the Christian is *faithfulness*. And faithfulness is the result of a disciplined life focused on the Kingdom of God. Nothing comes easy. Real success and true happiness are the result of a faithful, yielded, and disciplined life.

As God's Word says, you must seek first His Kingdom and His righteousness. Then, He will allow all good things to come to you. (See Matthew 6:33.)

God's Laws For Success

Certain laws and principles must be put into practice before you can experience success and abundant living. The spiritual and mental-emotional laws of life are far more important and exacting than the physical laws. "For bodily exercise profiteth little: but godliness is profitable unto all things, having promise of the life that now is, and of that which is to come" (1 Timothy 4:8).

God's laws can be tapped. Respect them and apply them to your life because with God all things are possible. Put these principles into effect in your life:

(a) *Hold a wholesome reverence for the Lord.* "The fear of the Lord is the beginning of wisdom: and the knowledge of the holy is understanding" (Proverbs 9:10).

(b) *Understand the depth of God's love.* His perfect love will cast out all fear—past, present, and future. (See 1 John 4:7.)

(c) *Act one step bigger than you presently feel.* Allow your faith to be exercised. "I can do all things through Christ which strengtheneth me" (Philippians 4:13).

(d) *Give freely to others as unto the Lord.* The "Law of Reciprocity" works on the principle of "what you give, you'll get." If you give to people what they need, you will receive blessings in return. (See 1 Corinthians 9:6.) If you have little love in your life, maybe you're not giving out much love!

The successful, abundant life is affected by:

What you think about. As a man "thinketh in his heart so is he" (Proverbs 23:7). One tends to do what one thinks about most.

What you act upon. Actions demonstrate and exercise your faith. "Faith without works (actions) is dead" (James 2:20).

What feelings you allow to dominate your emotions. You can choose to have positive or negative attitudes about any situation. Think about things that are true, honest, pure, lovely, and of good report. (See Philippians 4:8.)

The Formula For Success

God's Word is a critical part of the success formula. Joshua 1:8 says, "This book of the law shall not depart out of thy mouth; but thou shalt meditate therein day and night, that thou mayest observe to do according to all that is written therein: for then thou shalt make thy way prosperous, and then thou shalt have good success."

Without putting and keeping Scriptures in your heart, you cannot hope to achieve and maintain success in life.

"Blessed is the man . . . (whose) delight is in the law of the Lord; and in his law doth he meditate day and night," the Psalmist wrote. "And he shall be like a tree planted by the rivers of water, that bringeth forth his fruit in his season; his leaf also shall not wither; and whatosever he doeth shall prosper'' (Psalm 1:1-3).

Countless success stories appear in the Bible—some well known, others more obscure. One of the greatest kings of Judah was a man most people have never heard of: Uzziah. He is mentioned in 2 Chronicles 26:5: ''And he sought God in the days of Zechariah, who had understanding in the visions of God: and as long as he sought the Lord, God made him to prosper.''

Uzziah understood that a man's top priority was communication with the Lord. As long as you seek God, He will bless your life. There can be no success without communication with the Father. When you seek the Lord and keep Him in first place in your heart, then ''all these things shall be added unto you.''

Hebrews 11, the famous ''faith chapter'' of the Bible, talks about a variety of Bible characters who found the key to success. Noah is one notably mentioned. Compare the difference between his success as his neighbors saw it and as God perceived it. He spent decade after decade building a huge boat in his front yard and telling his neighbors that he was going to fill it with animals because it was going to rain. But Noah remained faithful, in spite of the strange looks and comments he must have received from those around him. Faithfulness, Noah knew, would bring success. His faith made him strong.

The day may come when you find yourself as alone as Noah was—in some position where nobody understands you. What will you do then? On whom will you lean? That's when you'll need to have these three elements of success ingrained in your personality:

(1) communication with God through prayer
(2) a working understanding of Scripture
(3) a faith exercised to believe God's Word

This life, with all of its problems, is God's way of allowing His servants to grow in faith. We can't see five or ten years down the road—we live day by day—and we live by faith.

Activating Successful Living

Happiness and success are attitudes of the mind. Don't let the fear of failure allow opportunities to pass you by. To attain a successful, happy lifestyle, you must begin living with a positive and happy attitude. I have called this process the *active personality reconstruction plan.* Start now to affirm the person you wish to become. You have the potential for greatness.

Let's put on the new man! Here is a three-step plan for "putting on" your new successful, happy, healthy outlook:

1. *Conceive success,* then confess success. See yourself as successful, and you will feel successful. Act successful, and you will attract successful situations and people into your life. As you are living

and performing in a positive way, you will have success.

2. *Conceive health,* then confess health. See yourself as healthy. When you are acting and thinking healthy, you will feel healthy! As you are living and doing healthy things, you will be healthy!

3. *Conceive happiness,* then confess happiness. When you are acting happy and thinking happy thoughts, you will feel happy. You also will attract rewarding situations and pleasant people. And as you are living and performing in a happy manner, you will have happiness!

Decide to be successful, happy, and healthy, then convince yourself of your decision! Dictate to your subconscious and don't let it dictate to you! Keep programming success messages into your subconscious. Ignore its messages of failure until the mind is completely reprogrammed and the messages it sends match the input you have been instilling.

Negative behavior and attitudes have been either *learned, caused,* or *goal-directed.* Often what you dislike in others, you see in yourself. You generally receive what you expect and believe is attainable:

(a) A mental image, plus action in faith, plus positive emotions results in positive attractions.

(b) You attract what you are emotionally prepared to receive.

(c) What you plant you'll grow. What you give out, you'll receive.

Faith takes the action-step forward and puts Hebrews 11:1 into practice: "Now faith is the substance of things hoped for, the evidence of things not seen." Faith, grown in the attitude of consistent faithfulness, lays the cornerstone for successful Christian living.

Developing A Plan

God wants the spiritual, mental, physical, educational, financial, social, and recreational areas of your life to be in proper perspective. But things can easily get out of balance. A workaholic who spends twenty hours on the job and sleeps only four puts too much emphasis on the financial and too little on the physical, social, and recreational areas of life.

Balance does not happen automatically. It must be planned. You must form a plan of attack for your life, asking the Lord to give you direction. You achieve planned balance by setting goals in every area of your life.

A plan is hatched in the heart. Then, as you believe it, faith takes over and makes that plan concrete. But none of this can happen without the first step: *the plan must be developed.*

Most people never set life goals. That's why they have no sense of accomplishment by the time they turn 60. They have not set out to accomplish anything, so they haven't accomplished anything!

In a way, people are like sharks. The shark has no mechanism for pulling water and oxygen into his body, so he has no choice but to keep swimming, forcing the water and oxygen in. People, too, must move forward, or they will die. This is why so many people do not live long after they retire from work. They suddenly have no purpose in life, no work to do, no mission to accomplish. Like a shark that stops swimming, they die.

Newton once said, "Growth is the only evidence of life."

Life in Christ is called the Christian "walk" because it's supposed to take you somewhere. If you have no direction or goals, you have no Christian walk!

As you take that first action-step in faith, following God's leading, the Lord will start changing things around on you. He will bring various elements of His plan for your life into sharper focus, so you can see more and more clearly what His overall plan really is.

The Wish Book

Immediately following graduation from college, a friend of mine married, expecting to get a job in publishing. The job Steve had been promised fell through, however, and he had to take a job in construction. But he continued to do some freelance writing on the side. After a couple of years of this, he realized he wasn't going anywhere because he had no clear idea of where he wanted to go! Steve began to think about what he wanted in life, in terms of spiritual growth, material goods, finances, career, and so on.

He made a scrapbook with several pages sectioned off into the various categories. On the cover, in a tongue-in-cheek gesture, he wrote the title "Our Wish Book." On the first page inside, he placed pictures of himself and his wife.

In each section, Steve filled the book with pictures of his "goals," clipping pictures from magazines and catalogues. Pasted in were such items as a new car, appliances, a house (he and his wife were renting), a family, a dog (white), a new typewriter, office equipment, and several other items that symbolized his goals for a career and financial assets. He encouraged his wife to include clippings, which she did reluctantly, thinking it was silly.

In addition, Steve wrote goals for their spiritual life. He wanted to establish a daily time of Bible study with his wife and become more involved in their local church.

Several times a week, Steve would browse through his wish book, reminding himself of his goals, occasionally adding or deleting certain items. He also prayed over his book as he looked through it. After a few months, however, the book was forgotten and stuck away on a shelf in a closet.

Within a few years, Steve came across the book while sorting through some boxes. He sat down and began to flip through it, astounded at what he discovered!

Looking through his "wish book" and thinking back over the past few years, he was amazed to realize how many of his "wishes" had come true! Although they had been made to happen through his own hard work, the "wish book" had provided the incentive.

He and his wife owned their own home and had purchased a new car. They had, after trying for many months, finally been blessed with a beautiful son. They even had a dog—a white one! Plus, they had better jobs and had grown spiritually through reading God's Word. They were actively involved in their church and ministering to others.

What had seemed like a silly and even futile exercise in wishful thinking had been an excellent lesson in visualizing specific goals. Without realizing what he was doing, Steve had programmed his subconscious to line up with his conscious desire for success.

Present-Tense Goals

What kind of person would you like to be five years from now? That is your five-year goal. Hold that image in your mind, and you will find yourself becoming that person. Your personality will actually change.

Write down your goals and think about them in the present tense, not in the future tense. Don't say, "I want to be a lovable person." Say, "I am a lovable person." This could be your goal for the spiritual realm.

For the physical realm, your goal could be: "I have many talents." You may be convinced that you don't have many talents, but God sees you in the fullness of your *potential.* God can use you in ways you don't even understand yet.

A suggested goal for the habitual procrastinator: "I'm going to do it *now."*

Are you regular in your prayer life? This is a good goal for any Christian: "I start every day with prayer."

Do you complain? Change that by setting a new goal: "Instead of complaining, I praise."

Set goals in every area of your life.

Do you have an educational goal? You can get a degree from a Bible correspondence school in five years by spending only 30 to 45 minutes a day in study!

Do you have a recreational goal? Determine to have someone over to your house once a week, or once a month, to demonstrate to your children what Christian hospitality is.

Many people go to counseling sessions year after year without seeing any change in their lives. Why? Because they haven't taken inventory of their lives and decided what they want God to do in them. They aren't standing still—they're in a spiral, spinning downward and growing more depressed each day.

Someone has said, "You've got to see it, then seize it, then say it." Imagine it first, grasp it by faith, and then confess it with your mouth. According to Scripture, "Out of the abundance of the heart the mouth speaketh" (Matthew 12:34).

This is why people who poor-mouth themselves don't get anything done. "I'm no good, I can't do anything," they say. So they don't do anything—they can't because of their negative confession. They are playing and recording and re-recording their mental tapes with negative garbage!

Erase your negative tapes and record over them by reciting positive, balanced goals everyday. Visualize attainment of your goals. When you read them, imagine them as fully accomplished and operative parts of your lifestyle.

Your success will increase step by step. You'll see a little bit of progress first, then more and more as time goes by. Each new area of progress will enlarge your faith, and with more faith you'll be able to step out further, scoring larger successes.

Making Goals Happen

Most of us have goals, even if we are not aware of them. To make your goals useful, you need to formulate them clearly and put them into writing. By "seeing" your goals in writing, you can direct your actions accordingly. This will help you avoid doing things that will take you off course. Written goals keep you from becoming sidetracked or delayed in your quest for a happy and successful life. Without goals and planning, you will end up either doing nothing with your life or spinning your wheels and burning yourself out doing the wrong things.

All of life is a series of choices. Your final destination is a by-product of the free-will choices you make every day and every minute of your life. By programming your mind and will in the right direction, God's perfect will can come into sharper focus in your life. A focused will is a powerful tool when brought into alignment with God's will. You can help direct your final destination by being focused on a daily basis.

Written goals provide specific guidelines for you to follow, but that does not mean they cannot change. As you grow in your walk with the Lord, your goals may be redefined. Changing direction is not an indication of failure but of progress toward a better understanding of God's will for your life.

At the end of this chapter is a life outline for you to use in writing goals. Take the action-step today toward a directed future by making goals in all the areas indicated. When you have completed your life outline, sign it, trusting the Lord to help you reach the goals you have set. The Holy Spirit will guide and direct you in accomplishing the objectives you wish to obtain.

Read the goals you have written out loud three times each day. In two or three months you will begin to convince your subconscious mind that you mean business. You will begin to feel the bubble of hope welling up in your heart as God's Spirit begins to reawaken your dreams and reconstruct your personality. What follows is so fantastic that it is beyond explanation. Get started and keep trusting God by continuing to hold nothing but pure, powerful optimism in your heart, never doubting. It works!

Five years from now you will be able to look back and see your life full and overflowing with fruit because you set out today to achieve that goal. Through goal-setting, you can become the kind of person who has such power with God that people will actually see it in your countenance.

Take fifteen minutes each day to have a *faith-believing period.* Shut yourself in with God.

First, praise Him.

Second, worship Him.

Third, wait for His peace to fill your soul.

Fourth, thank Him for yesterday.

Fifth, confess your goals out loud.

Sixth, relax and envision your goals as reality. Enter this period peacefully, shutting out distractions, and you will be richly surprised at the answers that come.

Dear Jesus, I know you love me and want me to succeed. Your Word says, "no good thing will be withhold from them that walk uprightly" (Psalm 84:11). I bind the spirit of poverty and accept your blessing on my life and relationships.

Help me, Lord, to discern your will and fulfill your purpose in my life. I need you in the center of my affairs and in the heart of my personality. Help me to abide daily in your presence so I can be fruitful in the work you have given me to do.

I commit my goals to you and ask you to help me accomplish them. May the Holy Spirit guide and direct me, bringing my objectives in line with your will for my life.

You promised that if we seek first the Kingdom of God and your righteousness, all other blessings will be added to us. I claim this promise for my life today. Amen.

Points To Remember

1. Measure success by your willingness to obey what God is calling you to do.
2. Success for the Christian is *faithfulness*. And faithfulness is the result of a disciplined life focused on the Kingdom of God.
3. Faith, grown in the attitude of consistent faithfulness, lays the cornerstone for successful Christian living.
4. Choose worthwhile goals and work toward them.
5. Write down your goals and think about them in the present not the future tense. Visualize attainment of your goals. When you read them, imagine them as fully accomplished, operative parts of your lifestyle.
6. Without goals and planning, you will end up either doing nothing with your life, or spinning your wheels and burning yourself out doing the wrong things.
7. Through goal-setting and follow-through you can become the kind of person who has such power with God that people will recognize Him in you immediately.

LIFE OUTLINE

	1 YEAR GOALS	5 YEAR GOALS	FINAL DESTINATION
SPIRITUAL:			
MENTAL:			
PHYSICAL:			
SOCIAL:			
EDUCATIONAL:			
RECREATIONAL:			
FINANCIAL:			

I entrust these goals to the Lord, believing He will enable me to reach them.

Signed_____

Chapter 10

REALIZING YOUR POTENTIAL

What is growth? *Growth* means God Rewards Our Willingness to Trust Him. God can do anything by Himself; He doesn't need anybody. In spite of this, He chose to use us to build His Kingdom. But we must be willing to step out by faith. God rewards our willingness to trust Him. It is the greatest form of growth available to mankind.

How many times have you been held back by unbelief? How many times have you allowed others around you to experience the victories and blessings that could just as easily have been yours? It doesn't need to be this way.

Unbelief is an abomination to God. Small thinking is not God's ideal. Repeat this out loud: "Small thinking represents small faith." Don't be quick to say anything is impossible. Instead, remember that the Scriptures encourage you to know you can do all things through Christ who strengthens you! The Bible is full of examples that show us God delights in doing the "impossible"—so put Him on your team.

Nothing lives without faith, for without faith it is impossible to please God. All of us must live by faith. God requires that "the just shall live by faith" (Romans 1:17).

Do Christian leaders live by faith and have vision? Sure, they do! They must. This is God's principle. They have to believe for larger facilities, greater congregations, more funds, better equipment, loyal people, and so on.

If you are not called to full-time ministry, then you should become the very best in your secular calling. If you are not called to be a pastor, evangelist, teacher, prophet, apostle, or counselor, then allow your life to demonstrate God's practical principles wherever you are planted.

To own nothing does not necessarily indicate greater spirituality. The Bible tells us that it is important not to be slothful in business. God's Word also says that he who does not work should not eat.

Blessings come to those who are willing to be obedient, pay the price, and then dedicate themselves to perform good, honest work. Money and physical blessings are a by-product of services rendered. They are a measuring stick and often indicate a person's concentration, dedication, and productivity at getting any particular job finished.

Taking Responsibility For Your Success

One night I had a dream in which I saw myself working in a vineyard. Nearby there was a house filled with joyous Christians. As I approached the house, I became a little envious of the good fellowship they were sharing. I wanted to put down my rake and go in. Suddenly, I realized that it was not my calling to be in the house, but I was to be out in the field doing my work.

Satisfaction comes from knowing what your personal responsibilities are and carrying them out.

One day a man came to my office complaining about his lack of success. To Bob, life was a proposition of "them" against "me." He even imagined that his inability to hold a job was due to persecution for "serving the Lord."

This type of person believes his life's calling is "martyrdom." He views all poverty and misfortune as "suffering for the Lord." Unfortunately, he often finds what he looks for.

Bob was brought up in a Christian home but rebelled against his parent's lifestyle. While living away from home, he indulged himself in the art of seducing girls by first telling them the gospel, then taking them to bed. Whenever rebuked for his ludicrous behavior, he called this "persecution" for his faith!

On the job, Bob was never prompt to arrive but was no stranger to the exit. He often would phone in sick and many times took off on compensation for a "back problem."

Bob's basic attitude was, "When I find a job I really like, then I'll work harder; but until then, they are lucky to have me working for them at all."

Life owes him a living, he believes. He never hurts others, they only hurt him, he rationalizes. "Why don't they love me?" he cries. He does not ask, "Why don't I love them and think about their needs." His own personal actions and attitudes have become totally self-centered, but he can't see it.

A person like Bob is always cursing life and God for not giving him a better chance. It still has not dawned on him that his life is a *choice*. Because he doesn't work and gets paid accordingly, he believes he is somehow holier than the successful, aggressive businessman who enjoys a richer lifestyle.

Bob has a mystical concept of Christianity. It is impractical and poorly grounded. His negative attitudes have paralyzed him at his level of living—spiritually weak and unstable.

Growth is essential at every level of life. We can't blame the past for present free-will choices. If I choose not to love, I will not receive love. If I choose not to forgive, I will not be forgiven. If I choose to condemn, I will receive condemnation. If I choose to curse my life, I will never succeed.

Success And Hard Work

It is not enough to know all the rules for goal achievement; you must act on them. These principles, accepted in faith and acted upon, are like having an automobile parked in the driveway full of gas. It is ready to take you in any direction you desire; you only need the knowledge or skill to operate it and away you go! Never be so foolish as to sit back and expect God to "do His will" without your willingness to mobilize yourself.

I remember that old television program from the early sixties called "Dobie Gillis." There was a beatnik on the show named Maynard. The character was a lazy, high school dropout who never applied himself to anything. When asked whether he'd like to work or not, he'd gag out the word "work" as though he were suffocating at the mention of it.

Many people in our society today are more than willing to let the system support them. Their numbers have multiplied more than ever before. Surely, this is not God's idea of greater spirituality. God's desire is that we should continue to put ourselves in the position where we will need to trust Him but not become slothful.

For the business executive, a little financial tension only tends to keep his instincts razor sharp. He can push himself to greater goals and steps of faith and enjoy seeing God answer his prayers again and again. His faith is in operation, so it increases. Conversely, the less one does, the less one wishes to do.

After years of working hard to help people in my practice, I was given the opportunity to purchase a demo luxury car at a price I could not refuse. When Sunday came, I drove my beautiful, new car to church. "How would people react?" I wondered, hoping they would not feel intimidated.

At the end of the service, I was standing by my new car near the church exit. One of the deacons, who happened to be serving on the board with me at the time, stopped his car and called out, "Hi, Doc! That's a beauty!"

Feeling a little nervous at being confronted so soon and directly, I exclaimed, "Thanks. God sure has blessed me!" This cliche was an assurance that God and I were still good partners, in my mind at least.

Then my friend, the deacon, responded with a comment that I have meditated on for a long time: "Yes, God has blessed you. But He's gotten a lot of hard work from you, too!"

When a person gives time, money, love, and hard work, he receives blessings in return. This is God's law! When the blessings follow, it is not God testing you. It is His reward for obeying His laws.

Blessings from God don't float out of the sky. If a person has no goals, he'll never do anything. When we discipline ourselves to work and to give to others, then His blessings will return to us.

Some folks pray, then sit and wait for the answer to arrive in the mail in some mysterious way. Others expect the clouds to part with a giant hand reaching down to them with a blank check. It is true that God sometimes uses mysterious ways to bless His people, but we are not to expect such interventions on a regular basis. God has the reserves and truly desires to fulfill our dreams, but faith without action is generally fruitless. Do all you can in a situation and then ask God to bless and anoint your efforts.

The Wise Investor

Are you still waiting to see God bless you? Remember that faith without action is dead. One way to put faith into action is by giving to the Lord's work. Tithe to God the first fruits of His blessings to you; bring your tithes and your offerings into His house and give to His service. (See Malachi 3:10.) Offer back to the Father a portion of what He has given to you, doing it with a joyful heart. Then wait for the blessings to begin flowing.

Good businessmen wisely recognize an advantage when it comes to them, and they waste no time acting on it. Colonel Harlan Sanders tithed to the Lord's work before he held any strong religious beliefs. Later, as the success of his Kentucky Fried Chicken made him a millionaire, he had the God-given wisdom to know that prosperity and celebrity status were not enough in life. He handed over the balance of his life to God Almighty, became a respected believer, and enjoyed many more years of good health and prosperity.

Would you hesitate to give a multimillionaire five dollars if he contracted to multiply it's worth and return it to you? Of course not. Yet, He who owns "the cattle upon a thousand hills" (Psalm 50:10) is again and again being denied the opportunity to prove Himself in this way.

If your church needs thousands of dollars for an expansion program, don't give just one dollar and pray for God to bless it. If a neighbor is in desperate need, don't draw away from him and wish him luck. Try giving what is required of you—your tithes—and be willing to give above and beyond with your gifts and offerings. You cannot out-give God; prove it to yourself.

Ability And Availability

The way God answers prayer is never predictable. We are to depend on Him, to trust that our goals and efforts are in line with His nature, and to stand by with a willingness to obey. Our talents are not as necessary as our willingness. A man without talent who is totally surrendered to God's will can accomplish much more than a talented man who doesn't know how to properly utilize what he has been given.

God is not looking for *ability* as much as He is looking for *availability* in those who serve Him. If you are doing what you feel you have been given to do in life—great evangelistic work or serving as a sales clerk—be thankful. Never stop dreaming, but allow yourself to be His hands extended wherever you are right now!

Never underestimate your abilities or become discouraged that you are not a great evangelist winning thousands of souls. Maybe you are a taxi driver who will one day witness to a passenger who will become that great evangelist. If so, you will share in the reward given for those souls being won. Be available no matter what you do.

Ethel Waters has stated, "God don't sponsor no

flops." How true. Believe in yourself as the wonderful creation you were meant to be and work with Him as your partner. Give Him the credit for your successes and merely regroup if you experience any form of setback.

Some people are always looking for God's perfect will for their lives, but they are unable to pinpoint what it is. Just get started, and expect Him to direct your ways. It is easier to change the course of a canoe once it is in the water than to try to move it on dry land. So jump in and get your feet wet. Man chooses his path, but God directs his steps. (See Proverbs 16:9.)

The Right Perspective

We live in an insecure world. Life does not hold guarantees. We have no security in the economy, friends, or jobs. Security is a learned response or belief that what was accomplished successfully yesterday can be repeated with relative ease tomorrow. Security is the belief that the fear of the future is a relatively small issue.

We've heard the expression that it's difficult to teach an "old dog new tricks." Why? We initially grow old in our minds. When we surrender to fear, failures, and losses, we choose to grow old emotionally.

This change can take place very early in life. It does not necessarily have to follow a chronological pattern. When a man admits he'll never be anything more than what he presently has become, he may age overnight. Or the moment a female believes there are no more opportunities to find her ideal mate, the aging process becomes obvious.

Put into perspective the free will choice to surrender to life. Start looking for new goals and creating a fresh outlook. It may mean taking a chance; but without a little tension, life becomes uneventful and boring.

God wants you to trust Him to accomplish great things in your life. But first, do all you can to choose a vision and set goals. Then, concentrate on your vision until God puts the whole jigsaw puzzle together.

Moving Beyond The Comfort Zone

Some performers experience "butterflies" before going on stage. I, too, have had these same butterflies when called upon to try a new task or challenge. Originally, I didn't like the sensation, but then I realized that this was a unique feeling. By accepting a new challenge, my whole system became alive and vibrant in the anticipation of what new things were about to be accomplished. I was "up," and I was involved! Not only that, but I was in God's hands, totally dependent upon Him to bless my faith in His ability. The result was not self-effort but a cooperative effort with God Almighty.

At different times in my life, I have been thrust into new situations that initially made me feel uncomfortable. However, by being willing to push myself beyond the comfort zone, I found the thing I least wanted to do or become has turned out to be my greatest discovery in life.

Life is exciting when we are challenged. Life means nothing without challenge. New careers, new speaking opportunities, new projects—all these keep us involved in life. Stay involved. Never be content to look at life as having a full belly and enjoying leisure time.

You do not conquer in life by fearing the problems associated with your dreams. You do not attain to the stature of a George Mueller by shrinking away from a challenge. Mueller's heart was stirred to build a home for orphans during hard times in England. His desire, coupled with a trust in God's ability to see him through, grew and grew until 2,000 orphans were under his care. As his dream expanded, so did the Father's provisions. A vision became a reality because he dared to step out in faith. And God was there!

Man needs to be self-actualized to be truly content and happy. Unless your own personal challenge or vision is stretched and pushed beyond the limits of comfort, you may never see the full potential within yourself. God has intended it that way; He is our Creator, and no one knows you in the intimate way He does. Your faith involves Him in your life, and without faith it is impossible to please Him.

Letting God Be God

The Lord loves to see us in the position of needing Him to intervene on our behalf. Then miracles can happen, and we learn to trust Him in a fuller and deeper way.

The first time I was asked to speak before a Christian group, I felt very inadequate and inexperienced. I was sure the old pro's I'd be addressing would easily see my deficiencies. I cried out to God to help me. "God," I prayed, "you must intercede and move through me. I can't do it on my own. God, I need your hand to rest upon me and let your presence be seen." In my weakness and vulnerability, I realized God would have to perform a miracle. He did, and He has time and time again.

Live, not by your own strength and abilities, but by putting yourself in the position where God can supply His power. As you do this, you will find yourself becoming more and more the complete, whole person God intended you to be.

Points To Remember

1. Blessings come when you are willing to be obedient, pay the price, and then dedicate yourself to perform good, honest work.
2. God is not looking for *ability* as much as He is looking for *availability* in those who serve Him.
3. God wants you to trust Him to accomplish great things in your life. Choose a vision and concentrate on that vision until God brings it to pass.
4. Unless your own personal challenge or vision is stretched and pushed beyond the limits of comfort, you may never see the full potential within yourself.

YOUR MAINTENANCE PLAN

To maintain your newfound personality in Christ, put these principles into action:

1. Dethrone sin immediately. (See 1 John 1:9; Romans 6:6.)
2. Resolve conflicts by making a decision. Be of one mind and conquer double-mindedness. "A double minded man is unstable in all his ways" (James 1:8).
3. Have a regular faith-building period with God and daily renew your mind. (See Romans 12:2.)
4. Seek wisdom and common sense from the Lord. (See Proverbs 3:21.)
5. Bring into captivity every thought to the obedience of Christ, thereby creating a controlled, Christ-centered personality. (See 2 Corinthians 10:5.)
6. Deny the validity of external problems by realizing your authority over them. (See Ephesians 6:16.) If the problem is external, give it no emo-

tional energy. Realize something is always going right!

7. Reclaim your inheritance from Christ, and stand against the giants of doubt, worry, fear, and negativity. They will rob you of your place in God, if you let them.

8. Realize the fruits of the Spirit are your inheritance. (See Galatians 5:22-23.)

9. Understand that you are special to the Lord. Move out continually in faith. Discern the good and acceptable will of God and realize the ultimate positivity of the gospel of Christ. (See Romans 8:28.)

10. Keep in mind that God corrects the child He loves. You learn by negative feedback so you can change your direction.

11. Learn to be dead to self. Become alive to Christ and allow His glory to radiate through your yielded life.

12. Remember that the sign of full surrender to Christ is your ability to express love. (See 1 Timothy 1:5.)

13. Remind yourself that God has not given you a spirit of fear, "but of power, and of love, and of a sound mind" (2 Timothy 1:7).

Renunciation And Affirmation

As a symbol of your new-found personality reconstruction, sign this commitment to release the past, live fully in the present, and face the future with hope and courage.

Read the following statement out loud, and then sign it. Also, have a witness present to hear your confession of faith and sign it with you.

Whenever you feel Satan's influence, when the past comes back to haunt you, or when you sense fear trying to pry back into your heart, read this document out loud again. Hold it up in Satan's face as evidence that you are not his, that he has no power over you, and that you are and intend always to be God's child and servant.

This document represents your renunciation of the pain of the past. It is also your affirmation of the joy of God's healing and the hope of the future in the Lord.

A Declaration

I, _____, as God's redeemed child, bought by the blood of Jesus Christ, my Lord and Savior, do here and now renounce, disclaim, and release myself from the mental, emotional, and spiritual sins of my ancestors and my past.

I announce that I have been delivered from the power of darkness and evil, and that I am now an heir to and part of God's holy Kingdom. I cancel all demonic working and influence from my heritage and past. I have been spiritually crucified with Christ and raised to live in newness of life and peace. Therefore, I cancel by the grace of God every curse that may have been put upon me through sin and evil workings.

By my own free will and in union with Jesus Christ, I claim my authority over all the works of the Enemy. I declare myself to be a joint-heir to all rights, freedoms, and power found in the name of Jesus Christ.

I renounce all external, negative forces and circumstances from having any control over my life or personality. I disclaim all authority in the name of Jesus Christ. I refuse to allow Satan and his evil thoughts, philosophies, and fears to ever bind me again.

All this I declare and do in the name and authority of my Lord Jesus Christ.

(See Mark 16:17-18; Acts 1:8; Romans 8:37; 2 Corinthians 5:17; Galatians 3:13; Ephesians 1:3; Colossians 1:13; Philippians 4:13.)

Signed _____

Witnessed by _____

ABOUT THE AUTHOR

At his Family Health Clinic, Dr. Norman Cawfield is concerned with meeting the needs of the *whole* person. Over the years he has seen hundreds of people healed and restored by the principles of personality reconstruction.

His radio program, *Real Living,* airing from Buffalo, New York, reaches a wide audience in the United States and Canada. As a result, Dr. Cawfield receives many requests to conduct *Real Living* seminars in churches and conferences. He has also been a guest on the popular *100 Huntley Street* television program.

In addition to being a Doctor of Chiropractic, Dr. Cawfield holds a doctorate in Christian ministry and a Master of Divinity degree in Christian psychology and counseling.

"Dr. Norman Cawfield is a man of compassion who has prepared himself spiritually and academically to be a fine-tuned instrument in the hands of God. His deep desire to see people enjoy life to the fullest in spirit, soul, and body is evident in the many lives he has helped. He has a wide range of experience dealing with people in the most intricate and complex areas of their inner person. This qualifies him to share on the subject of God's reconstruction plan for your life."—Rev. Ralph Rutledge, host of *Revival Hour* television program.